Wicked Northern New York

Wicked Northern New York

Cheri L. Farnsworth

The History Press

Published by The History Press
Charleston, SC 29403
www.historypress.net

Cover images: Portrait of John Van Buren from the Brady-Handy Collection. *Library of Congress Prints and Photographs Division;* "The Hasty Burial," by Antoine Wiertz. *Wikimedia Commons;* Photograph of a man seeing triple by Strohmeyer & Wyman. *Library of Congress Prints and Photographs Division;* Man on horse taken by Pinkerton's National Detective Agency, circa 1900. *Library of Congress Prints and Photographs Division.*

First published 2011
Second printing 2013

Manufactured in the United States

ISBN 978.1.60949.305.9

Library of Congress Cataloging-in-Publication Data

Farnsworth, Cheri, 1963-
Wicked northern New York / Cheri L. Farnsworth.
p. cm.
Includes bibliographical references (p.).
ISBN 978-1-60949-305-9
1. Upstate New York (N.Y.)--History, Local--Anecdotes. 2. Upstate New York (N.Y.)--Biography--Anecdotes. 3. Rogues and vagabonds--New York State--Upstate New York--Anecdotes. I. Title.
F126.8.F37 2011
974.7'1--dc23
2011024493

For N and A

This one's for you…gypsies, witches, hobos and all.

Eat, drink and be merry for tomorrow we shall die.
—Imhotep (2655–2600 BC)

Photograph by Strohmeyer & Wyman, 1897. *Library of Congress Prints and Photographs Division.*

Contents

Preface

While I was able to locate several photographs of the actual individuals and places involved in the following stories, this book is mostly illustrated with images of *unidentified* people who best represent each chapter. I left no stone unturned trying to find more before coming to the conclusion that, had this book been exclusively about sensational murder cases or disasters occupying the pages of local papers for an extended period of time, there may have been images available. But *Wicked Northern New York* is, for the most part, a potpourri of lesser evils (horse thieves, body snatchers, gypsy swindlers, tramps, prostitutes, etc.). And because such stories were somewhat common in newspapers of the day, they rarely warranted the publisher's added expense of illustrating them. Besides, it would have been difficult to try and pin down the transient beings, like gypsies, women of ill repute and wild men, who star in this crazy cast of characters long enough to do an engraving or even take a photograph—especially when the guilty parties were often told to leave town on the next train in lieu of jail time.

Therefore, I carefully selected the following images from my own personal, fast-expanding collection of early photographs and postcards, as well as from the Library of Congress Prints and Photographs Division and the vault of images at Wiki Commons. Captions will indicate where each image came from. I hope you enjoy the stories *and* the pictures as much as I enjoyed compiling them for you.

Acknowledgements

I'd like to thank my commissioning editor at The History Press, Whitney Tarella, and senior editor Jaime Muehl for their continued enthusiasm and expertise. And many thanks to the New England sales rep, Dani McGrath; Jamie-Brooke Barreto of sales and marketing; and my publicist, Katie Parry, and assistant publicist, Dan Watson. I always know I'm in good hands with them.

Special thanks to Laura A. Foster, curator, Frederic Remington Art Museum, for helping me obtain the coveted image of Ameriga Vespucci. And thanks to Ann Werley Smallman, executive director of the Franklin County Historical and Museum Society; Margaret Gibbs, director, Essex County Historical Society/Adirondack History Center Museum; Kaleigh Ratliff, collections assistant at the Essex County Historical Society; Michele Tucker, librarian at the Adirondack Research Room in the Saranac Lake Free Library; and Amy Catania, executive director of Historic Saranac Lake for taking the time to search their files. Sincere gratitude also goes to the Northern New York Library Network for digitizing the region's newspaper archives in its Northern New York Historical Newspapers database and to the Library of Congress Prints and Photographs Division and Wiki Commons for doing the same with countless historic images.

I was blessed to come from a family of authors, songwriters, musicians and artists who not only gave me the genes and the drive to create but also provided me with the best support network anyone could ask for. For that, I thank my parents, Tom and Jean Dishaw, as well as my sisters, Cindy Barry and Chris Walker, and my brother, Tom Dishaw. And I can never possibly convey how grateful I am every single day for my daughters—Michelle, Jamie, Katie and Nikki. As the song goes, they fill my world with gladness…

Most of all, I thank my wonderful husband, Leland Farnsworth II, who has always been tremendously understanding and supportive of what I do. He knows all too well what this calling of mine entails (with his own background in the literary field), and he's got my back.

Introduction

Wicked means a lot of things to a lot of people: evil, sinful and mischievous; severe, dangerous or foul. In slang, it can have positive connotations, denoting something that is really awesome (as in "wicked cool"). And, while I hope this book *is* wicked cool, the true stories chosen to best represent the title have to do with the sins of our ancestors, the vices and failings of human nature (greed, lust, apathy, ignorance, revenge, etc.) and the deeds borne of wickedness that inevitably breed lawlessness. In the early North Country, there was malice, like when a Potsdam man named Griffin was tricked into a pistol duel with a surprise ending in 1817 and when Mrs. Covey, an alleged adulteress from the town of Fine, was stripped naked, tarred and feathered by an angry mob as she stepped off a train with her mother and brothers in 1895. There were chilling abductions, like that of Mrs. Miller of Parishville, who was snatched from her bed in the early morning hours and dragged off into the night in a flimsy negligee in 1812. Her skull, with the chiffon gown wrapped around it, was found about four years later, tucked into a fissure in a cliff side several miles from her home. Freddie Brosseau was only six years old when he went missing from the Potsdam area in 1896. Incredibly, seventeen years later, he escaped from his abductors and found his way to a monastery near Montreal, where his family was summoned to confirm his identity; and a little girl in Clinton County was taken by gypsies around 1908, following the death of her mother and abandonment by her father. She was then sold to a proprietor of a house of ill repute for a paltry fifty cents, and he traded her to an abusive man for a half dozen chickens. The disappearance of a Stockholm man named Daniel Murdock was made even more bizarre by the fact that he appeared to have risen from the dead. It was reported that the young man tasked with tending to the corpse until the next morning's funeral fled the house only moments before the body went missing, when the familiar birthmark on the neck of the deceased reappeared, as if he were awakening.

There were plenty of greed-driven crimes back then, like the father-son team of body snatchers who robbed fresh graves of their corpses in the mid-1800s so they could sell them to medical schools in Montreal and anywhere else. Because the field of medicine had exploded, there was a great need for such covert operations, and the business proved lucrative to the infamous Gilmans, who are buried in a lonely field near Trout Brook in Stockholm. The mysterious hermit of Maple Island had bags of gold (of unknown, potentially shady, origins) when he arrived in Clayton seeking a remote island hideaway for reasons unknown to the few residents he spoke to. Nobody would ever learn his true identity because he was murdered, and the bag of gold was taken, perhaps by its rightful owner, one stormy night in 1865. But nowhere did the lure of easy wealth make as big of an impression as it did to the shoreline directly across the river from Treasure Island, just off Hawkins Point in Louisville in 1842. Generation after generation dug into the earth there for forty-five years, based on the advice of a psychic girl from Watertown and a prominent pillar of the church named John Power, who had a dream about the fabled buried treasure. The dig site became known as the "money hole," but no wealth was ever found. Of course, Treasure Island and the entire "money hole" site have long since been submerged with the construction of the Seaway and Power Project in the 1950s, which flooded the area in question. And that means that if there truly *was* any buried treasure, it may still lie buried somewhere on the river bottom.

Countless houses of ill repute infiltrated the region, and a white slavery boom in the early 1900s had young French-Canadian girls crossing the border into Ogdensburg and Plattsburgh in droves, lured by the promise of job opportunities that would ensure them "nice clothing." Punishment, if one was caught being associated with a house of ill repute, included banishment from town (and agreeing to never return), deportation back into Canada, jail sentences, lectures on morality and fines. In at least one local case, the combination of lust and liquor had lethal consequences. A young man named Allen Mooney, of Saranac Lake, became so drunk and so jealous that he opened fire in a house of ill repute on election night in 1902, injuring his rival and killing his love interest and her friend, who was in the next bedroom. His actions (which he swore he couldn't recall the next morning) earned him a date with the electric chair at Dannemora.

Besides the crimes of greed and lust, we had the mother of all wagers when Madam Vespucci was "won" in a game of cards. We had all kinds of wild-man sightings (the kind with long hair and scant clothing that terrified women and young ones). We had tramps (and even a Tramp Camp, if you can imagine). We had gypsies passing through the area continually for some thirty years, telling fortunes and robbing folks of their money (and kids). And we had thieves. I'm talking nationally acclaimed outlaws, like Franklin County's sweetheart of horse thieves, Lon Clark, who stole one hundred of them at last count. Other stories I've selected to share include the Native American girl alleged to have had an evil eye, with the ability to turn milk sour just by looking at it, and the Potsdam man whose wife died from the "excitement" of her final beating. Rather than blame the blood clot in her brain on the smack her husband landed upside her head, her death was deemed the result of apoplexy caused by excitement. Truth really is stranger than fiction.

Yet for all these misdeeds, no individual seemed sorrier for his human frailties than the man who chained himself to two trees deep in the woods of North Hudson and threw away the keys. He had set out to fast for forty days and forty nights, like Jesus, so that the devil would leave him alone. He died an unspeakable death trying to atone for his sins. He may have been deranged, but at least the wretched fella had a glimmer of conscience—and that's more than I can say for some of the people you're about to meet.

The Day Mrs. Miller Was Snatched from Her Bed

Parishville, 1812

Among the early settlers of Parishville were brothers Stephen and William Miller, who built their log cabins from the trees they felled while clearing their lots in 1811. They lived with their young wives in a thriving little settlement on the northeastern corner of town, near a hamlet called Beechertown, straddling Parishville, Stockholm and Hopkinton. It was here in this peaceful wooded community that a vengeful brute of a man named Hugh Biggan terrorized his estranged "wife" and neighbors and took one of the Miller women off into the night.

While the Millers lived just inside the Parishville border, Biggan lived on the other side of the border—within a stone's throw from the Millers—in the town of Stockholm. He allegedly came from Canada, accompanied by a hapless young woman he passed off as his wife. She had actually been kidnapped and was being held against her will, as a *Courier & Freeman* article from 1916 explains:

> *It was said that he had been in a Canadian prison when the War of 1812 had broken out and had been released to fight for the king. One night on picket duty, rumor had it he had bayoneted a fellow sentinel to death and had fled to the St. Lawrence, forcing a girl whom he found alone at her home to row him across the river and then to accompany him on his wanderings.*

With a criminal past like that, it's no surprise that Biggan found himself in more trouble with the law soon after arriving in Beechertown. What his infraction was is anyone's guess, for no record stating the offense remains.

But when he was sentenced, he swore to get revenge on his "wife," his neighbors and especially on Mrs. Miller for testifying against him. (The articles referenced didn't specify which Mrs. Miller.) Because he swore to get even with the girl he claimed was his wife, we can speculate that perhaps she confided in Mrs. Miller that she had been kidnapped, and for that, Biggan was arrested. Or perhaps the girl accused Biggan of assaulting her, and Mrs. Miller testified on the girl's behalf. Either scenario would explain his determination to seek revenge on both Mrs. Miller and his alleged bride. And seek revenge, he did.

In late October 1812, Biggan broke out of jail and returned to his old neighborhood in Beechertown, as promised. Biggan's so-called wife had been staying with some kindly neighbors, who provided both comfort and support. On October 23, there was a loud knock on the door of their cabin, and—as fate would have it—the girl went to open it. Just as she did, an axe blade ripped through the darkness, grazing her forehead and embedding itself in the door casing. The attacker fled into the night, and while everyone soon suspected it was Biggan after learning of his escape from jail, the girl said it was too dark to tell and that everything had happened too fast for her to be sure. Everyone in the household stayed awake that night with worry, and with good reason. A bit later, someone stuffed dry straw under the eaves of the cabin and set it on fire. While the women threw water on the flames, the man of the house stood guard with his gun. The intruder, whom everyone suspected was Biggan, was still at large, and all of the residents of Beechertown were on high alert, especially Mrs. Miller. By then, word had reached Beechertown that Biggan, the escaped convict, had been seen crossing the Racquette River, presumably on his way back to the settlement. Mrs. Miller was so worried that he would come after her that Mr. Miller left his loaded rifle with her and told her to keep the door to their cabin barred. Two nights later, on October 25, her worst fears became a reality. According to the *Potsdam Herald-Recorder*:

> *In the course of the night, she awakened her husband and told him that she had heard a sound as of someone snoring or breathing heavily. He listened but heard nothing and credited her alarm to overwrought imagination. In the morning he arose as usual and, finding the fire had gone out, went to their nearest neighbor's* [his brother's house]*—only a short distance—to procure some live coals. Upon his return, he found Mrs. Miller had left the house, but seeing nothing unusual, and noticing that her shoes and stockings and some other garments remained as left the night before, he did not at once feel any*

Courtesy of the author.

> *uneasiness. But after some time had passed, and his wife did not appear, he began making some search and passing around the house, he found under the window on the outside, opposite where the bed stood in the room within, a place where the weeds had the appearance of having been pressed down by some person lying close up to the logs of the house. He alarmed the neighbors, and a search was started for the woman and her supposed abductor or assassin.*

So that was how Mrs. Miller went missing, dragged barefoot and probably gagged (or someone would have heard her scream) across the frigid ground, wearing nothing more than a thin negligee on a cold October morning. When Mr. Miller had left to get coal just moments before, she was still in bed and had not yet dressed. Her day clothes were still lying on a chair by the bed when he returned and found her gone. And her abductor also took Miller's rifle, which he kept on a hook above the fireplace. Evidently, Mrs. Miller didn't have a chance to grab for it before the ruthless assailant was upon her. Miller alerted his neighbors, and all the men of the settlement set out with their guns in search of his missing wife. But without snow, there were no fresh footprints to track, and the *Courier & Freeman* said "every dog in the place had been poisoned with arsenic sometime in the night," which sounds a bit improbable. Still, that's what the papers said. To make matters worse, while the whole town continued its search for Mrs. Miller over the next few days, Biggan somehow managed to set fire to several barns in the neighborhood. He must have disposed of her before returning to wreak more havoc. Four days after the woman's disappearance, Biggan was spotted in the western part of Parishville. The *Courier & Freeman* said:

> *A few days later he was arrested at Carthage, evidently having crossed the Adirondacks by the old Indian trail leading from the headwaters of the Racquette across to the Cranberry Lake country and down thro' the "Level Belt" tract to the "High Falls" of the Black river* [sic].
>
> *He was brought back to Ogdensburg for trial, but his "wife" could not swear that it was he who tried to kill her,* [and] *there was no direct proof he had carried off Mrs. Miller or burned the barns. He did not have Miller's rifle in his possession, but did have another stolen from a house near the Racquette ferry. For this theft, he was given a long sentence at Albany prison, where the following winter he died.*

For several years, no trace of Mrs. Miller was found, and with Biggan gone, having never confessed before he passed away, nobody knew what had become of her. Then, one spring day several years later, a man named Wolcott Morse was logging about four miles north of Parishville and had let his oxen stay out through the night. The next morning, they were nowhere to be seen, so he climbed up on the ledge of a boulder to get a better look at the surroundings. The *Courier & Freeman* said:

> *Glancing into a cleft in the rock, he discovered what had the appearance of being some article of clothing. He procured a pole with a hook at the end and reached into the fissure, which was about ten feet deep by only two wide, and after some difficulty, drew out the cloth* [later determined to be a nightgown] *and found wrapped therein a human skull. Further search resulted in the discovery of other remains which were identified as those of the unfortunate Mrs. Miller.*
>
> *The assassin had died unconfessed, and there was none to tell the story of the terrible journey which the woman took before meeting her fate; but the rational explanation is that, having lain in wait all night awaiting an opportunity,* [Biggan] *had compelled her to go with him, on foot, barefoot and scantily clad through seven miles of trackless wilderness, subjecting her to such torture as his malevolence suggested, then carried out his murderous design; and, still unsatisfied, had wantonly mutilated the body.*

Morse carried the skull, nightgown and other bones back to the settlement, where they were identified as Mrs. Miller's. But that night, three years after Biggan's passing, Morse's logging fires inexplicably started a blaze that consumed the whole logging area, including the fissure in the rock where he had found Mrs. Miller's remains. He couldn't recall where he had found the items because the charred surroundings looked so different. From the day Biggan set foot in Parishville, there had been a series of unfortunate incidents such as this. Then, one hundred years later, a sportsman named Alfred J. Sayers stumbled on a wedding ring believed to be Mrs. Miller's, and the whole tragic tale was recalled.

Painting by D.A. Goltz. Postcard by W.R.R. & Co., Wien, Illinois. *Courtesy of the author.*

Sayers was fishing for trout on the upper St. Regis one warm, sunny day in June 1916 and had scooted up to higher ground in a little cleft in the rocks to eat his lunch. That was when a glint of gold in the moss caught his eye. Reaching for it, he saw that it was a "little golden circlet," according to the *Courier & Freeman*, "still showing the chasing of clasped hands borne by old-time wedding rings." Not knowing about the mysterious disappearance of Mrs. Miller a century earlier and how important it might have been to mark the location, Sayers had no reason to make note of exactly where he stood. But the discovery of the wedding ring in the general vicinity where Morse found Mrs. Miller's skull and nightgown was, according to students of early St. Lawrence County history in 1916, the "closing scene of an atrocious and mysterious crime." Now, nearly two hundred years later, details surrounding the mysterious abduction and apparent slaying of Mrs. Miller remain sketchy at best.

The Last Laugh

Fall Island, Potsdam, 1817

Long ago, where the ancient Trinity Episcopal Church on Fall Island has stood for over 175 years, a pistol duel was fought, and the loser was made a fool, even as he struggled to blurt out his final words of endearment and instruction to those standing over him, laughing. He was the victim, alright—the victim of a practical joke but not of a fatal gunshot wound. There was little for the early St. Lawrence County settlers to do to satisfy the basic human need for entertainment. The things we take for granted today—television, the Internet, malls and movie theaters—didn't yet exist. So the fledgling communities springing up across the North Country found other ways to amuse themselves. According to L.H. Everts in his early *History of St. Lawrence Co., New York*, "practical jokes were the order of the day," and the famous Oscar-worthy Fall Island duel was "perhaps the most exciting one."

About 1817, a man named Speers visited the shop of a watchmaker named Griffin on Fall Island. He was looking for a new watch, and—making casual conversation—asked the busy watchmaker what he was using to clean the watch pieces. Griffin told him it was acid but that it was harmless, and he dared him to take a sip. In fact, he told Speers that if he was man enough to drink it, he would give him a watch for free. Speers accepted the dare, taking in a mouthful of acid and silently holding out his hand for his reward. The stunned watchmaker gave him a watch, as promised, never realizing that Speers had turned his head and spit out the acid when Griffin wasn't looking. (I don't know how he missed such a spectacle, but he did.) Speers left the shop wearing a new watch…and a smug grin.

It didn't take long for word to get around about the stunt. The locals thought it was pure genius and took it as a personal challenge to try to top it. A couple of men hatched a plan that would teach the watchmaker a lesson for offering acid to unsuspecting patrons, while at the same time providing an afternoon of entertainment for the little community. They would convince Griffin that Speers had become terminally ill from the acid he ingested and that Griffin would be hanged for prodding Speers to drink it. Then, they would offer the horrified watchmaker a way out of his predicament—and if all went as planned, they would then hold title to the most impressive practical joke of all time (at least around here). According to Everts, poor Griffin begged them to help him, to which the pranksters said, as solemnly as they could muster:

> *Well, Speers is able to be up yet, though the doctors say he is sure to die. You had better challenge him to fight a duel. That is a fashionable thing among gentlemen, and if you kill him, you will never be punished. But if he dies of the poison you have given him, you will surely go to the gallows.*

Courtesy of the author.

Griffin saw little choice but to agree to a duel, kicking himself all the while for having pulled such a foolish stunt as he had in the first place. He could never have imagined that his momentary lapse in judgment could lead to another man's demise—and now possibly his own. Speers, who was already in on the joke, eagerly accepted the invitation, and the two masterminds of the plot designated themselves as the "seconds." In most duels of yesteryear, each party was assigned a trusted person to be his second. Besides offering moral support, the second's job was to choose a suitable location for the duel (where they wouldn't be interrupted) and to check that the pistols to be used were acceptable to both sides and that the duel was fair in all respects. The offended party—in this case, Speers—traditionally got to choose what would constitute a fulfillment of the duel. The options included stopping the duel as soon as one man was wounded, regardless of how minor the wound; ending the duel when one or the other was physically incapable of continuing; stopping the duel only when one or the other was mortally wounded; or stopping the duel after a single shot was fired by each man, even if both missed their targets. In fact, oftentimes, both men purposely missed their targets under the single-shot rule and walked away with their honor and dignity still intact. In this case, the duel was over when one man only *believed* he was mortally wounded.

On the morning of the Fall Island duel, Speers and Griffin arrived at the intended site with their seconds, preceded and followed by a large crowd eager to see the show. After all, it wasn't every day that a duel was fought in their town. Everts said:

> *The parties appeared, each provided with a second and a big horse-pistol, while a crowd of the villagers collected to see the fun. The seconds loaded the pistols with powder only, placed their principals in position, and then one of them gave the word:*
>
> *"One—two—three—fire!"*
>
> *Fire, they did; but, of course, without inflicting any injury. Again, the pistols were loaded with powder, again the word was given,* [and] *again the fruitless shots rang out for the amusement of the chuckling spectators. At the third fire, Griffin's own second, who had stepped up behind him unseen, struck him a tremendous blow with his fist and felled him to the ground. The unfortunate duelist thought he was shot, and the sympathizing bystanders assured him that he was not long for this world.*

Crying, Griffin hastily offered instructions on how to dispose of his belongings as he bid those around him a hasty, heartfelt farewell. It must have pained him to see them laughing at him as he lay dying. Finally, as the laughter subsided, someone explained to the poor watchmaker what had happened. The bad news was that they had played a cruel joke on him. The good news was that he wasn't dying, and neither was Speers. Griffin had been punched by his second as part of the prank, they confessed. *Punched*, not shot. His second had smacked him at the very same moment the third shots rang out, making Griffin *think* he had been shot. The watchmaker was so overjoyed to learn that he and Speers would both live that he treated the crowd to a gallon of rum. And that's entertainment North Country style.

The Woman Who Was Won in a Game of Cards

Evans Mills, 1841

The John Hoover Inn at 8497 South Main Street in Evans Mills was built by the man for whom it was named, a captain who was stationed at Sackets Harbor during the War of 1812. With all the colorful history an ancient inn like that surely accumulates, nothing would ever compare to the time when a beautiful young woman of prominence was wagered in a game of cards. On a chilly January night in 1838, one man's loss became another's serendipitous good fortune. The famous players in this wicked tale were George Parish II, John Van Buren (the president's second son) and Contessa Helene America, as she preferred to be called (even though she was baptized "Elena" Vespucci). Mostly, though, she went by Ameriga Vespucci—*Madam* Ameriga Vespucci.

Parish was a wealthy Ogdensburg businessman and the young brother of Baron von Leftonberg of Saxony, whom he would succeed in 1856. He had come to the United States to represent the banking house of Hope and Company of Amsterdam and set up residence in the Parish Mansion on Washington Street. Madam Vespucci arrived in America in 1838, seeking citizenship and a grant of land in the Washington, D.C. area on which to settle. She allegedly came to America after being ordered to "break off an intimacy with the Duke of Orleans, eldest son of [king of France] Louis-Philippe, and leave the country." According to an article in the *Sunday Herald* on August 8, 1897, Vespucci was "young, radiant and beautiful, with all the charm of birth and breeding and the glamour of foreign courts about her." In R.R. Madden's *The Literary Life and Correspondence of the Countess of Blessington*

Ameriga Vespucci. *Courtesy Frederic Remington Art Museum, Ogdensburg, New York, Public Library Collection.*

(1855), she was described as being "of fine features, symmetrically formed, of the perfect Italian style of beauty, with more of Juno's characteristics than of Venus's peculiarities in its excellency. Her figure," the book said, "was commanding, full, strongly set up, and finely moulded." And her eyes were dark and "wonderfully brilliant," complementing "hair, black as jet and of extraordinary length and abundance."

As a direct descendant of the famous explorer Amerigo Vespucci, after whom our continent was named, and an ancient noble family of Florence, the madam expected to be treated like royalty wherever she went in her worldly travels, simply by the drop of her name. It worked—at least for a while. After all, there was something about the Italian beauty that people of blue blood and high society could not resist. Her friend, the Countess of Blessington, explained:

Madame Vespucci's conversation is original and amusing, full of animation, abounding in incidents of travel, highly interesting and graphic when descriptive of scenes or people of distant lands she is familiar with. She possesses a certain wild, unsteady energy and cleverness. She is naturally restless, unsettled in religious opinions, of a romantic turn, of intense vanity, being tormented with a constant desire to excite attention.

And excite attention she did. But the real reason Vespucci had come to the United States was soon revealed, and hushed talk of the amour between her and John Van Buren did nothing to dispel the rumors. According to the *Herald*:

All seemed to be going well for the "fair Florentine" when the tongue of scandal, which had all along been whispering protests against her unconventional acts, began to talk openly of her intimacy with "Prince" John Van Buren, son of the President and a noted Albany lawyer and stump speaker. It was reported that she had borne an unenviable reputation both in Florence and Paris and had been induced by a pecuniary consideration to break off an intimacy with the Duke of Orleans, eldest son of Louis Philippe, and leave the country. Soon after, the Duke's younger brother, the Prince de Joinville, came to this country and refused to recognize her, which virtually excluded her from respectable society. She retired from Washington to Albany, where "Prince" John Van Buren's name was still associated with hers. Soon after, she accepted the protection of Mr. Parish, Baron von Leftonberg.

The madam's sudden fall from grace among the rich and famous (and pompous and judgmental) in Washington, D.C., prompted a hasty move to Albany, New York, where the Honorable John Van Buren (aka "Prince" John after his famous dance with the queen of England) lived and practiced law. There Madam Vespucci remained, until the day she accompanied Van Buren on a business trip up north. The illustrious couple's arrival in the North Country, according to the *Herald*, went like this:

A big sleigh drawn by four fine horses came floundering through the snow drifts from Rossie and drew up at Capt. John Hoover's tavern at Evans Mills. One of the fur-coated occupants of the sleigh was a man of most kingly bearing, young and noble looking, faultless in dress and with every mark of blue blood and breeding. He was George Parish of Ogdensburg… Mr. Parish ordered a fire built in the fireplace of the old dancing hall,

Honorable John Van Buren, circa 1855. *Brady-Handy Collection. Library of Congress Prints and Photographs Division.*

> *and three chambers to be prepared, as he expected to meet Lawyer John Van Buren of Albany there on business connected with his estates in that vicinity. About noon the famous lawyer arrived, driving through from Utica in a sleigh. He did not come alone, however, but was accompanied by a woman, tall, stately, and handsome, who was magnificently dressed and who wore a profusion of jewelry. She spoke with a foreign accent and was introduced by "Prince John," who was a tall, stately and fine-looking man, as Madam Vespucci…It was noticeable, even to the bartender who served them, that George Parish was much more deeply interested in Van Buren's fair companion than he was in his legal lore, and that the interest was mutual.*

Van Buren drank heavily that day, according to sources, before excusing himself for a bit just before dark, leaving Vespucci to carry on a conversation with Parish. When he returned, he invited Parish to play cards and proceeded to lose all his money. Realizing he had nothing left to wager, he decided that the $5,000 in gold he had just received from a client as an investment toward property would have to do. Sack by sack, he lost it all. And perhaps noticing the easy camaraderie developing between Madam Vespucci and the Ogdensburg land baron, Van Buren suggested that the madam might want to "follow the gold." She refused, telling Van Buren that she would only leave him if he *made* her go. There are two versions of what transpired next. In one, the gracious Parish offered to "put up the $5,000 and as much more with it," win or lose, if the winner could keep the madam. The trio apparently agreed to the unusual wager. Parish won that hand of cards—and the woman. When he handed Van Buren the promised money, the lawyer refused to accept it, so Madam Vespucci tried to offer it to him. Still, Van Buren refused, telling her to hold on to it for the day when her "beauty faded or her friends failed."

In the other version, Van Buren had lost over $5,000 and was down to his very last gold coin, when he made a proposition to Parish, saying, "I shall play you the lady against my losses, Mr. Parish…on the toss of my last gold piece." Regardless of which version is correct, Van Buren lost, bid the destined couple farewell and headed toward Boonville, while Parish and Vespucci "drove away through the starlit winter night toward faraway Ogdensburg and the brick-walled villa that was to be their home for the next sixteen years." The baronial mansion still stands in the form of the Frederic Remington Art Museum.

Parish and Vespucci never married, but she was considered his longtime mistress (to the displeasure of some of the locals, who felt the couple was living in sin). In 1856, Parish's brother passed away, and he was summoned by family to return to Germany and assume his title of Baron von Leftonberg. He was also told that he must marry a "daughter of nobility" and break off his stateside relationship with Ameriga Vespucci. Bowing to the demands being placed on him, he had no choice but to leave her. Two years later, the madam returned to France, and the *Herald* said she left "a lonely, sad, and heart-broken woman, who but for her folly might have left a glittering instead of a clouded name upon the pages of history."

Frankly, I believe the *Herald* got it all wrong. I think Madam Vespucci most certainly *did* leave an impressive mark—a "glittering," if you will—on the pages of history, at least in the annals of North Country lore.

Treasure Island and the Fabled Money Hole

Wilson Hill, Louisville, 1842

In 1842, on the advice of a young Jefferson County psychic, a party of Louisville residents commenced a treasure hunt of epic proportions in search of Lord Jeffrey Amherst's supposed "cache of gold." Although they already knew of Amherst's disastrous voyage through the rapids of the St. Lawrence, the psychic offered them something history texts and hearsay hadn't: an exact location of the buried treasure.

It all began in 1760, according to the same story told and retold in countless local newspapers over the years. That year, Lord Amherst and his army meandered their way along the St. Lawrence River in "the conquest of Canada." The fort at Chimney Island was captured, as was Father Piquet's settlement at Ogdensburg. At the time, the Long Sault Rapids just below Treasure Island were considered one of the most dangerous sections of the uncharted waters. So Amherst decided it would be wise to bury a large chest of gold in a safe location near the river and pick it up later, after a safe passage through that area was found. The last thing he needed was to have the gold lost in a shipwreck when his men were counting on it for their very survival. According to a number of news articles, "The Sault actually proved a burial spot for many of Amherst's bateaux [as he had feared] and a large number were drowned." Among those who drowned were the men chosen by Amherst to take the gold secretly into the woods and bury it in a safe place. They were allegedly the only people who knew where to find it.

The legend was revived in 1842, when a Louisville resident had the same identical dream three nights in a row regarding buried treasure. He and his

Sketch by Howard Pyle, 1887. *Wikimedia Commons.*

neighbors were convinced that it was an omen. The papers said, "In brief, the dreamer saw a chest of gold in a familiar spot on the banks of the river; and on his approaching it, a ghostly voice said, 'Do not touch it. It belongs to John Power.'"

Well, wouldn't you know, John Power was a prominent Louisville citizen and a pillar of the church, and although he *said* he felt as if the "fates were thrusting [the unknown wealth] on him," he felt it was his duty to seek advice from his church "brethren" and determine their next course of action. To support his dream, they consulted a psychic; after all, "only superstitious people followed dreams without question," according to the *Observer*, which reported:

> *So they called to their aid a young woman, famed as being gifted with "second sight." She was born with a caul over her face and was said to be able to locate lost articles, tell the whereabouts of absent friends, and do diverse and sundry mysterious and unaccountable things. She was brought in from Watertown and went into the dark cellar of the house of Robert Crawford…and gazed into a looking glass. There, she saw a chest of gold and described its location exactly as had been seen in the dreamer's dream. She was supposed to be an entire stranger and totally unacquainted with the locality and surroundings. She guided them to a spot on the bank of the St. Lawrence…directly opposite Treasure Island.* Still *there were skeptics,* [so] *an expert with a divining rod was brought into service. He passed over the ground many times, his instrument always pointing unerringly to the spot located by the dreamer and clairvoyant.*

With much excitement and all doubt removed, having divined the same information from three unique sources, the treasure hunters began to dig into the frozen December ground near the shore of the St. Lawrence in 1842. While many of their Louisville neighbors could appreciate the task at hand, there were those who sought to sabotage the treasure hunters' efforts, and they did this each Sunday, when the devout (like Power) were at church. The troublemakers would open a ditch between the excavation and the river and allow water to rush in, requiring the gold seekers to pump it back out before continuing. By March, a hole that was eight feet deep had been dug all the way down to the bedrock, supported by planking around the sides. Still, no gold was found. Hopes were dashed, and tired volunteers passed the torch on to new seekers year after year, but not an ounce of gold was ever found there. The dig site became known as the "money hole" because of the time, effort and resources put into the project—not because of any riches it yielded. Eventually, the plank siding rotted away, and the ice gorge of 1887 finished the site off once and for all.

It would appear that the psychic, the water witch and the dreamer were all wrong, at least insofar as *where* the chest of gold was buried. Perhaps the gold was buried somewhere else in the vicinity, like Treasure Island, which now lies beneath the surface of the St. Lawrence. It would certainly make more sense to bury it in a place more difficult to find than along the well-traveled Louisville shoreline.

Treasure Island was so named by Miss Mary Bradford, the daughter of Captain Henry Bradford, who lived on the road along the river near Ogdensburg. She knew of the legend associated with that location—about nine miles below Waddington and opposite the town of Louisville—and the name seemed appropriate. For years in the early 1900s, a group of Ogdensburg businessmen calling themselves the "Treasure Island Club" made the island their home, using it as a campground for their exclusive club during the summer months. An *Ogdensburg Journal* article from 1954 said that the members were required to remain on the island for three full weeks, with no contact whatsoever with the outside world. This exclusive group included doctors, mayors and other local men of prominence. When the Seaway was built and the St. Lawrence River was flooded westward from Massena, their summertime playground, along with any aspiration of finding the long-lost treasure on the island, was dashed. Treasure Island (and, perhaps, Amherst's fabled chest of gold) were submerged about six hundred yards off the northwestern shore of Wilson Hill.

The Day Daniel Murdock Rose from the Grave

Stockholm, 1850s

I've heard some crazy things, but never have I heard of a corpse vanishing from the casket it was laid out in the day before the burial. Yet that's just what happened in Stockholm in the 1850s, when a mysterious stranger left the area in as puzzling a manner as he had arrived. The setting was an old one-and-a-half story, stone farmhouse set back on a ridge some distance from the highway on a sharp bend of the St. Regis River, where the river flows into the town of Lawrence. Because the farmhouse, owned by a Mr. Doud of Malone, sat on a fairly rugged and secluded lot, the townspeople were used to it being vacant much of the time. But *someone* found that very isolation appealing. When the farmers in the neighborhood noticed one spring that they had a new neighbor in the old Doud house, naturally their curiosities were piqued, especially since something didn't seem quite right about the silent newcomer. They would have to get the scoop from Mr. Doud.

The three-year lease on the property was signed by a man named Daniel Murdock, the neighbors were told. Based on his "speech and dress and his wagon and farm tools," according to the *Republican-Journal*, they felt he was a Canadian. The middle-aged man had a distinct "great scarlet birthmark" on his throat and was "of morose and forbidding countenance," they later recalled. And, clearly, he wanted to be left alone. The papers, retelling the tale of Murdock, said that the bachelor kept a "scantily furnished home" and that his "crabbedness soon caused him to be left, as he evidently desired, to himself." But there was one man who occasionally paid him a visit—a brother named David Murdock, who looked so much like him that he could easily pass as his twin. When the two were together in public one day, they were overheard talking about being among the "California gold seekers of [1849]" and that Daniel still held claims from mining that David apparently hoped to use as security for money advanced.

Daniel Murdock did all of his farming alone, unlike his neighbors, who often swapped work. By all accounts, he was a very hard worker who preferred doing the bulk of his work in the field by lantern light, while the rest of the community was sleeping. Nevertheless, he was surprisingly productive, and—other than his peculiar antisocial behavior—there was really nothing about him with which his neighbors could find fault. By the time he was found dead three springs later, he had actually started to grow on the townsfolk.

One warm spring day, Aaron Fortune was passing by the Doud property where Murdock lived when he noticed something dangling inside the barn. It was Murdock; he had hanged himself. Fortune cut the body down and sounded the alarm. According to the *Ogdensburg Advance*, "Soon the farm house had more visitors than it had seen in many a day." Mr. Doud was notified and attempted to locate Murdock's only known relative, David, but when he couldn't be found, Doud made arrangements to have Murdock buried in the nearby cemetery. A large pine coffin was crafted by a Lawrenceville carpenter, and the neighbors prepared Murdock's body for a proper burial. It was then, as they draped the shroud over the dead man's body, that they noticed his distinctive birthmark had all but vanished from his throat. If they didn't know any better, they would have sworn it was his twin brother, as that was the only distinguishing feature that set them apart. Instead, they assumed the decolorization was a natural part of the postmortem process.

The body remained in an open casket for three days before the funeral. On the first night, two young farmers agreed to stay the night, followed by two different farmers on the second night. And finally, on the third night—the day before burial—Mr. Fortune (who had found the deceased in the barn) and a young schoolmaster named Eli Jones agreed to do their part and "watch" the body. The *Advance* of March 15, 1917, said, "Every two hours, according to custom then followed by such watchers, cloths wrung out in saltpeter solution were freshly spread over the face of the dead." About midnight, Fortune's wife became very ill, and a neighbor summoned him. Jones said he'd be fine alone with the corpse because "he wasn't afraid of ghosts"—or so he thought. In between the two-hour intervals, when cloths had to be freshly applied to the corpse, Jones hung around outside. At approximately two o'clock in the morning, he "crept back into the candle-lighted room to perform his dreaded task," and the *Advance* said:

"The Hasty Burial" by Antoine Wiertz, 1854. *Wikimedia Commons.*

> *When he removed the cloth, he saw with horror that across the throat, again the scarlet splotch* [appeared], *and with a shriek, he fled from the house and stopped only when he reached the Fortune home, half a mile away.*
>
> *In the early April dawn, Fortune, young Jones, and a neighbor returned to the silent house, where the door still stood open as left by Jones, with the candles flickering beside the sheet-draped table, but the corpse was gone, shroud and all. The coffin stood ready, the grave waited for an occupant, the country minister and bearers came; but there was no funeral, for the chief character was missing and was never located.*

There were many theories as to what became of Murdock's body on that strange, strange night. Some believed that it was a case of "suspended animation" and that the birthmark reappeared as the man returned to life. (Suspended animation is the slowing down of life functions to the point that a person appears dead, and his breathing and heartbeat cannot be detected.) Still, how many people survive being hanged? Nevertheless, those who toyed with that theory thought that perhaps Jones's loud scream at the sight of the birthmark had fully awakened the dead man and that he then fled into the night, back to Canada where he had come from, or "that when he was aroused by the shrieks of young Jones, the would-be suicide had fled to the river to complete the work he had [begun] with a rope." Others believed that his brother, David, finally heard the news and arrived to an otherwise empty house (coincidently seconds after Jones fled in fear), so he took his brother's body away with him to wherever the two of them had come from in Canada.

Another perhaps more plausible theory was that body snatchers, who were known to be operating in the North Country at the time, had been lying in wait for just such an opportunity to seize the fresh body to sell to medical schools in Montreal.

Nobody ever figured it out, and if the old house held any clues, they have long since been destroyed. The house was shunned by the neighborhood after the disturbing incident, and "a few years later," according to the *Advance*, it "burned down in that mysterious way that such old, unoccupied buildings generally do."

The Invasion of the Body Snatchers

Northern New York, 1800s

To rob a grave of jewels and personal effects is bad enough. But to dig up freshly buried bodies, unbeknownst to grieving family members who thought their loved ones were resting in peace, and sell the stolen corpses like hot commodities is beyond wicked. Back in the day, body snatchers sought fresh graves because the soil was still loose and moist and, therefore, easier to dig up. They would lay out a tarp to shovel the soil onto. Once they reached the coffin, generally six feet under, they pried open the lid and grabbed the corpse, sometimes removing the clothing and throwing it back into the casket. Then they would flip the tarp back over onto the grave when their task was complete, thereby keeping the area tidier and less suspicious. After securing the body, they would package it up (with a little ingenuity) or hand-deliver it to facilities in need of fresh, lifeless bodies for medical research, such as dissection, as a tool for learning the medical profession and for anatomy lectures.

Although the criminal practice of body snatching was considered unethical by most physicians—and they could never openly admit to their participation in such activities—it nevertheless thrived throughout the eighteenth and nineteenth centuries as medical schools began to flourish. And finding acceptable cadavers from traditional means (bodies donated to science for dissection, bodies unclaimed by family and bodies of felons who agreed prior to their execution to sell their corpse to the highest bidder) did not offer enough supply to meet the growing demand.

In the 1800s, there were sporadic reports of body snatching from every corner of Northern New York. In Clinton County, we had Dr. Erwin of Centerville, near Mooers, who caused quite a stir when it was reported that the body he was seen dissecting (with the assistance of a fourteen-year-old French boy) had been snatched from a local grave. The villagers were in a panic, wondering if the deceased was someone they knew, according to the *Plattsburgh Sentinel* of April 23, 1869:

> *This produced great excitement through all the west part of the town, and everyone who had recently buried friends were alarmed by fears that they were being subjected to the gross indignity of dissection in an old blacksmith shop...The Doctor replied that he had obtained the body lawfully and had a right to proceed with its dissection...*[so] *a complaint was made before F.P. Allen, Esq., against the Doctor and his student for robbing a grave. They were arrested and a lengthy examination held by Esquire Allen. Able counsel were employed in behalf of the People and the accused. Graves in which dear ones had recently been interred were re-opened by anxious friends to ascertain that their bodies had not been stolen.*
>
> *The result reached by the court was that no proof had been found to convict the accused of the charge, and they were discharged. The question, whose body was it?, is still unanswered, and the course of the Doctor in having a human body dissected by a French boy of 14, in so public a place*

Postcard from I.L. Maduro Jr., 34–46 Cathedral Square, Panama. *Courtesy of the author.*

as an old blacksmith shop by the grist mill and at the end of the bridge in the middle of the village is as mysterious as ever.

From Jefferson County, we have the story of Terry Connell's postmortem excitement. Old man Connell was laid to rest on February 21, 1898, in the cemetery connected to St. John's Episcopal Church in Cape Vincent, and two days later, body snatchers nearly got him. Edward Murray, who lived near the cemetery where the ninety-one-year-old man was interred, was heading off to work early at 4:00 a.m. on February 23 when he noticed two men in the back part of the cemetery with a horse and sleigh nearby. When the strangers looked up and saw Murray watching them, they immediately jumped into their cutter and sped off. Further inspection by Murray and others he notified revealed the disinterred body of Mr. Connell lying by the side of the road, "where they had dropped it in their fright," according to the *St. Lawrence Republican*. The *Watertown Re-Union* added further detail, saying:

There were evidences that the vandals had dragged the body to the fence, then thrown it over the fence and dragged it to the road and were about to put it into the sleigh when Mr. Murray's timely appearance scared the scoundrels away.

The grave robbers left their shovel and left the grave open. It is supposed the body snatchers came from Canada, crossing the river on the ice, and that the body was to be used for the purposes of dissection in the medical college at Kingston [Ontario]*...About two rods from where the body was found, tracks were seen where a sleigh, drawn by one horse, was turned. A new shovel of Canadian make was found near the open grave.*

Mr. Connell's body was cleaned, returned to the casket and placed in the vault, where it would be safe from vandals. As newsworthy as the Connell case was, St. Lawrence County harbored the most famous grave robbers in the area. The notorious Dudley Gilman and his son, John A. Gilman, lived beside Trout Brook in Stockholm in a settlement called Old Forge. They both worked in a mill that manufactured barrels, tubs and even crutches for Civil War casualties. The two were notorious body snatchers whose nefarious skills were in high demand throughout New York State. They dug up random fresh bodies, setting aside anything of value that they could pocket or sell in another town (so the stolen objects were less likely to be recognized), and they stuffed the bodies into barrels from the mill they worked at and shipped them off, via horse and wagon, to medical schools around the state, reportedly receiving up to $100 per body (nearly $3,000 today). They also dug up skeletal remains to sell to physicians and medical students for demonstration purposes and teaching (or simply as novelty items).

One *Courier & Freeman* article from 1938 said that neighbors became so fearful of the thought of body snatchers among them that they began to bury their loved ones beneath their bedroom windows to prevent or interrupt grave robbers from carrying out their nocturnal activities. They suspected the Gilmans. Realizing they were under suspicion by an angry populace, the father and son team gave family members very specific instructions about how and where to bury them, when the time came. They wanted their bodies placed in pine coffins and buried four feet below the surface in the middle of a field, far away from civilization, with alternating layers of straw and earth that they felt (through personal experience) would make it more difficult for other body snatchers, or I dare say, an angry mob, to find them.

Their wishes were granted in 1850, when the Gilmans were literally caught in the act of digging up a corpse. They were stopped in their tracks by neighbors who had long suspected, but never proven, what the men were up to—until then; and they were allegedly shot where they stood. As instructed, family members buried their kin in a lonely field about 250 yards across the road from their house on Trout Brook, in an area early news articles described as "near the Four Corners" and "only a stone's throw" from an old starch factory foundation. The stone slabs the family later set over the graves were laid flat, making them difficult to find by anyone but family members who knew they were there. The grave markers read as follows:

Dudley Gilman
66 Years
Almighty God, the ruler of all
Gods by thy just and mighty hand
that I did fall
If at thy right hand, I fail of a seat
I then would pray at Jesus feet

John A. Gilman
1850
In his 27th yr
We can't but hope that he's gone to rest
We trust in God who knows him best
We hope he's reached that happy shore
We here on earth shall meet no more.

Mystery Hermit, Eccentric Recluse or Hunted Assassin?

Maple Island, Clayton, 1865

In the spring of 1865, a weary traveler arrived at Fishers Landing looking for lodging. Because out-of-town visitors were few and far between, the locals took notice of him. The *Watertown Re-Union* of July 25, 1896, said the man was "very reticent and refused to talk of cities he had visited or say where his home was located. He had come over from Gananoque in a skiff, and this was the extent of the information regarding his arrival or antecedents." It was clear to those who listened that he was "well-bred and intelligent," and he seemed to have a southern accent. He was described as a well-dressed man of about thirty years with a dark complexion that complemented his black hair and whiskers.

For a while, he remained reclusive in the hotel he was staying at, never venturing far from his room, as if he were in fear of being recognized. Then one day, he announced that he was moving onto Clayton's Maple Island in the St. Lawrence River, effectively removing himself from society. On the island, he fashioned a hut from rough lumber with a six-foot-high ceiling and eight-foot-wide walls. Although it was only thirty feet from shore, passersby could not see the dwelling through the dense foliage and trees. To the hermit, it was the perfect hideaway, and the fewer persons who knew about him, the better. The *Re-Union* said:

> *He was an excellent musician, and many an evening the tones of his violin would float across the waters of the St. Lawrence, but no one was ever invited to his abode. It was known he had a good supply of books and was*

From the National Photo Company Collection, 1922. *Library of Congress Prints and Photographs Division.*

> *a man of unusual attainments, but apparently distrusted his fellow beings and shunned all friendly advances. The few necessities of life, he purchased of the farmers on rare trips to their settlements, paying for them in British gold, of which he seemed to have a plentiful supply.*

One stormy night in the fall of 1865, an intense fire broke out on Maple Island, and all along the shore word spread quickly that the hermit's hut had been struck by lightning, or so the river residents thought. Then, in the light generated from the flames, spectators noticed the silhouettes of three or four men scurrying about the island. The hermit was not alone. Neighbors assumed the others they saw on the island were helping the hermit—they assumed that they had all escaped the burning island—but they soon learned differently. The next morning, according to the *St. Lawrence Republican*, when nearby residents ventured over to the island to see if their reclusive neighbor needed help or shelter, they found that his hut had burned to the ground and his boat was missing. Then they discovered his body near the shore at the opposite end of the tiny island, about an eighth of a mile from where his hut had stood. The paper said his "head and body were literally chopped to pieces with an ax or other sharp weapon." Other news sources, like the *Watertown Re-Union*, reported that "his throat had been slashed from ear to ear, and on his breast was gashed three crosses in the shape of a triangle." The crosses were tilted to look like the letter *X*.

Such a display of crosses was a well-known symbol of the Knights of the Golden Circle, also known as the Order of the Sons of Liberty, a secret society founded to protect the interests of the southern states and fight for the right of any state in the Union to leave and create their own form of government. If such markings were truly carved into the hermit's chest, it was an important clue to his identity. The familiar bag of gold pieces from which the farmers had always been paid was missing. The hermit had been robbed and killed. After the coroner finished examining the remains, the body was buried "in the little strip of sandy beach on the northwest side near the foot of the island, and within fifty feet of his burned hut." In 1892, an area resident submitted the following letter to the editor, suggesting that the grave had been defiled:

> *In regard to the murder of the Maple Island hermit…I wish to say that I have since learned that a certain Wall St. broker, now dead, who some years ago owned a cottage, and a fast steam yacht, and who made himself and his gang notorious by their acts of lawlessness and drunk jamborees, went one day in the summer of 1877 to the place where the body of the unfortunate man was buried, and partially exhumed it, taking away the skull which they afterward took with them to New York, and had it made into a tobacco box. The rest of the bones, I believe, were left in the grave on the Island.*

No trace of the hermit's killer or killers was ever found, and nobody has ever determined who the men were that were seen running around the hermit's hut the night of the fire. However, a week before the murder, three unknown southerners had arrived in Clayton and rented a boat on the premise of taking it out for a late-day row on the day of the murder. When they returned late that night, they seemed "considerably excited," according to news accounts. The *Re-Union* said the men then hired someone to row them to Alexandria Bay, where the three split up and went their separate ways, never to be seen in the area again. A theory soon emerged about the hermit's involvement in a presidential assassination plot. The paper said:

> *It is a matter of history that an offer of $300,000 in gold* [over $4 million in today's dollars] *was made for the assassination of Lincoln, Grant, Sherman, Sheridan, Johnson, Seward and others, and that John Surratt was paid $100,000 in English gold at the Queen's hotel in Toronto. The sum was paid by "Jake" Thompson, at that time an agent for the confederacy in Canada. Surratt was accompanied by John A. Payne, a brother of the man who was hanged for the attempted assassination of Seward and his son. John A. Payne was known to be connected with, and the treasurer of, a Washington secret society. It is also a fact that Surratt and Payne left Toronto the night the money was paid to Surratt.*

Ultimately, based on all the facts gleaned from the investigation, authorities came to the conclusion that the hermit might well have been Payne. They believed *he* had received the money in Toronto that was to be shared with the other would-be assassins in the plot; but instead, Payne took the money and ran, fleeing to the Thousand Islands in hopes that he would never be found on an island as inconspicuous as Maple. There, the men he had duped hunted him down, killed him and left their mark, so to speak, on his chest in the form of a triangle of crosses. Payne, after all (if that is, in fact, who he was), had sworn an oath to be loyal to the secretive Knights of the Golden Circle, and he violated their laws by refusing to share the money received for Lincoln's assassination plot.

This theory was further substantiated when another recluse named Robert McAdam called his neighbor to his bedside shortly before he died to share the story of his life. According to the *Daily Journal* and the *Cape Vincent Eagle*, McAdam said that he, too, was a member of the same secret society to which Payne belonged and was in Toronto when Payne was paid $300,000 in gold, which he was to divide among others in the assassination plot. So McAdam was among those betrayed by Payne. The eighty-five-year-old man confessed that he was with the party that attacked Payne on Maple Island in 1865, for they belonged to the Knights of the Golden Circle, "the violation of whose oath meant death." By running off with the entire $300,000, Payne broke his oath to the Knights, "and death was meted out to him at his lonely home."

In 1914, the daughter of a woman named Jenny Hickey, who died in 1903, shared her mother's recollections of her time spent with the hermit of Maple Island, and her story corroborated the Payne theory. Hickey was once a dairy maid at the Rusho farm on Grindstone Island, one of the farms that sold staples like butter, eggs and milk to the hermit. She was often asked to take those staples to Maple Island to save the hermit a trip—as he was a good, paying customer. She didn't mind, for he was handsome and charming, and easy friendship blossomed between the two. They spent much time, she said, fishing and rowing together. According to the *Cape Vincent Eagle* of February 26, 1914:

> *Jenny was curious about the handsome stranger and his reasons for leading so lonely a life, and she begged him to allow her to see his cabin.*
>
> *When she visited the place, she plied him with questions, and, in spite of his evident intention to say nothing of the past, Jenny drew from him the information that he had fought in the war under Stonewall Jackson and Lee. He showed her a book containing Confederate war songs and pointed out one, a lament on the "Death of Jackson," of which he said he was the author. It was subscribed "John A. Payne"—and Jenny had his secret.*
>
> *The hermit became alarmed and charged her never to mention it, as it might cost him his life if his identity became known. Since Jenny knew so much, however, the man relaxed and told her more, showing her pictures of his friends. One of them was John Wilkes Booth. "He was my dearest friend," declared her host.*
>
> *Jenny asked if she might keep the pictures of himself and Booth, but the hermit refused, and then apparently forgot that the girl still held them in her hands and finally carried them away with her.*

A few days later, Jenny's father passed away, so she returned to her home in Kingston, across the river. At the same time, her fiancé, a sailor, returned home after a long voyage, and they were married. She never returned to the Rusho farm to work—or to visit her friend on Maple Island. Jenny told her daughter that she held on to the photographs of Booth and Payne, much to her husband's dismay, as she wouldn't tell them who they were. One day, he decided he'd had enough of the photographs his wife was so secretive about, and he threw them into the fire. Jenny reached in and grabbed them, but Payne's image had already burned away, leaving her with nothing but memories of the hermit of Maple Island.

Still, the Payne theory has been discredited by some who believe the hermit was actually a southerner named Godfry J. Hyams. Hyams was a former Rebel soldier who was appointed first assistant to the chief Confederate commissioner at Toronto. When he learned of the Confederate plot to burn down New York City the day before the national election in 1864, he told Federal authorities, giving them four weeks' notice. For his traitorous act, he received $100,000 in cash and fled. But on the train between Toronto and Halifax, where he planned to board a ship, he noticed that he was being watched, so he snuck off the train somewhere near Gananoque to hide out for the winter. In the spring, he found his way to Maple Island, where he would remain in hiding through the summer, keeping as low a profile as possible. According to the Hyams theory, he was murdered and robbed of his reward by those he betrayed.

While neither theory has been entirely substantiated or accepted by all, one point that everyone can agree on is that the hermit was a wanted man whose days were numbered, and he knew it. The mystery of the Maple Island hermit remains open to conjecture, and we will likely never know whom he wronged—whether it was the Knights of the Golden Circle or the Confederacy—or what he did to deserve such a terrible end.

Wild Men of Northern New York (the Hairy, Scary Kind)

1874–1948

Hermon, St. Lawrence County, has a sensation. A wild man is reported in the woods near there. Last Tuesday night a party went out to capture him. They found the nest of leaves in a hollow tree where the wild man had slept, and many tracks around it, but they have not at latest accounts caught any wild man. Those who have seen him describe him as very tall, with a beard reaching almost to his knees, and but very few clothes on.
—Daily Journal, *December 11, 1874*

Wild men were all the rage in the North Country of yesteryear, when you could count on a new cluster of sightings every other year or so. The *Daily Journal* was no stranger to reports of wild men. As early as 1869, the paper had become so jaded toward the topic that one article was simply titled, "Another Wild Man," as if the reporter were yawning as he wrote it. The article described the following tale (tall or not), which was told by one witness:

> *A party of men, while coon hunting on Thursday night last, about nine o'clock, two miles and a half above the Eel Wier Bridge, on the west side of Black Lake, were started up in a lively manner by a wild man. The party consisted of six persons, three men and three boys. They had been through a corn-field with their dog, in search of coons, and had taken a seat on the bank of the Lake, and were enjoying a quiet smoke. All at once, a man on his hands and knees came bounding out of some bushes, having*

been startled by the dog. The children were frightened terribly by the visitor and were hurried to a place of safety.

Thomas Carrol, one of the coon hunters, was caught around the legs by the wild man, who jumped upon his back and tried to bite him on the shoulder. After a severe struggle, Carrol made his escape and took to the cornfield. He was pursued, but by hiding in the corn, eluded the monster. Mr. Carrol described the wild man as a hideous, hairy monster. The affair has caused the most intense excitement in that neighborhood. The above information we gain from Mr. Carrol himself.

A creature covered in hair and running around on all fours sounds more like a bigfoot than the typical Joe Wild Man of those days. Did bigfoot roam the countryside of Northern New York in the 1860s? Usually, so-called wild men ended up being escaped criminals, escaped lunatics, hermits or tramps. Occasionally, an ape-like beast such as the one described above would get thrown into the mix, just to keep things interesting. Besides the Black Lake and Hermon wild men, there was a "wild man of the woods" named Robinson who, in 1880, was taken by a priest to Ottawa, where he could be placed in the House of Compassion. Not everyone shared the priest's desire to rescue such individuals from the wild. The *Plattsburgh Sentinel*, for example, stated on March 9, 1883, the "great scare at Port Henry is the wild man, who scares women and frightens the children. He appears at times in an overcoat, but cannot be traced or detected." And St. Lawrence County added another to its list of wild men in 1904, when the town of Benson near Fine became "excited over a supposed wild man in the Stony Brook district who looks fierce, wears long, uncombed hair and shoots into barns." The constable was directed to find him and arrest him, but it's unclear if he accomplished his mission. Wild men are inherently slippery creatures, like the following man reported in the *Ogdensburg Republican-Journal*:

A "wild man," clad only in a bran sack in which he has cut armholes, is terrorizing citizens in the vicinity of Brandon and Bangor. Parents have refused to allow their children to attend school. Even the dogs are frightened.

The "wild man" is said to carry a large club similar to that used by the cave man of old. He is said to have chased one boy and even threatened to kill him. State troopers, with a German police dog, tracked the man to the edge of a stream where it was thought he escaped by swimming. About 25 residents of the section continued the search after the departure of the troopers.

The man is described as being elderly with long gray hair and moustache.

"Wilder Mann mit Wappenschild," by Martin Schongauer, 1480. *Wikimedia Commons.*

The Adirondacks played host to a wild man who called a cave in the vicinity of Onchiota and Lake Kushaqua home in 1909. The few times he ventured out into daylight (and society), he was allegedly "terrorizing people with his raids and strange appearance." Lucky for the poor guy, after being caught foraging for food in dumpsters in the freezing cold, he was taken to the considerably more hospitable county jail for thirty days on charges of vagrancy. That same year, and not far south, the cave dweller settled in the Rainbow Lake area, creating much excitement over the course of three or four years and earning the moniker the "Wild Man of Rainbow Lake." The *Plattsburgh Press* of November 19, 1909, said:

> *Many stories are afloat about the appearance of this mysterious individual. One is that about two weeks ago, he jumped off a passing train, and has been hiding in the woods since that time. His lodge has been found in a hollow tree about a half mile from the railroad station. Many chickens have mysteriously disappeared, and numerous persons have been frightened by the appearance of a long-haired wild man. Sheriff Steenberge of Franklin County has been notified and urged to come and capture the individual, who is supposed to be a lunatic, before he does himself or others any injury, and before the weather becomes so severe that he perishes in the cold.*

The man, as it turns out, was John Hunston (aka John Coons and John Kunz). Hunston was captured and held in jail through the winter months of 1909–10 so he wouldn't freeze or starve. In 1911, true to form, he was arrested again and locked up for ninety days for vagrancy. The sheriff and the superintendent of the poor found him living in a crude shack made of logs leaning against a boulder; the structure was leaking profusely when they arrived. He had no shoes or food, and he appeared to be suffering from a mental breakdown, so back to jail he went until summer. In this way, Hunston always ended up in the nearest jail before the real cold set in, and that arrangement seemed to suit him just fine, especially with all the media attention and fanfare he received. Among wild men, he was a celebrity. The *Chateaugay Record* of February 16, 1912, said, "Hundreds of people have flocked to the jail to see him," when he took up his annual residence that winter. The paper, in describing his appearance, said it was like that of a man who was either wild or insane:

> *His hair was light brown and unkempt and his beard red, short and scrubby…Until the recent cold spell, he lived in a cave, it is believed… The man speaks in broken English. He says he came to New York City in 1884. Further than that, he would have nothing to say. He appears to be about 48 years old, of florid complexion, is five feet, eight inches tall, and weighs about 190 pounds.*
>
> *When captured, he had on a pair of shoes that weighed eight and one-half pounds, seven or eight pairs of trousers, three undershirts and three or four coats.*

He may have been slightly overdressed, what with eight-and-a-half-pound shoes and all, but at least he wasn't half naked and covered with hair, like some of the wild men spotted around here. And it was better than the year before when he was found shoeless in the winter. He was definitely more prepared for the weather than the wild man found nearly frozen to death in Keeseville in 1920. In that case, the tracks of a barefooted man were found in the snow, repeatedly circling an outbuilding on the property of Frank and Harvey Mussen, one morning in late November. The Mussens followed the tracks of the intruder through the snow and found their culprit lying at the foot of a tree in a swamp, unconscious, barefoot and nearly naked. The same man had been occasionally showing up on people's doorsteps in the area, begging for food before fleeing back into the woods. The *Essex County Republican* said the Keeseville wild man was "observed sneaking 'round various farmhouses, near the outbuildings, but evidently harming nothing and at the first sign of alarm would disappear as fast as his legs could carry him."

When found, the poor man was nearly frozen to death and was unable to communicate. His words were unintelligible, so authorities had no idea who he was or what his story was. All they knew was that they had found him in the nick of time. The deputy sheriff, of whom the man seemed particularly fearful, arrived, along with the village doctor, who said he believed the man would survive the effects of his exposure. Were it not for his feet being severely frozen, he was an otherwise healthy male. The only clue they had to his identity was in a bundle of old clothes he carried around with him. The sack contained letters and postcards written in a foreign language, with one addressed to a John Hola in Racine, Wisconsin.

The following year, a new wild man was reported in North Country papers; this time, he hailed from the hamlet of Skerry in Franklin County. The *Commercial Advertiser* of August 30, 1921, said:

> *The unknown wild man who has been roaming the forests and swamps near Skerry for the past ten days in search of whom large posses of men have been scouring the woods since last Saturday, still remains at large, and the mystery of his identity is far from being solved.*

The mystery of another wild man's identity a decade later was also never solved, but not because he eluded capture. It was because he was killed once he was located. In March 1932, an African American was shot and killed by a posse of four state troopers, a force of game wardens from Long Lake and two trappers in the remote Blue Mountain Lake area when he fired at them as they closed in. His untimely death resulted in a question that has never been answered: who was the "Wild Man of the Adirondacks," as he was dubbed?

Photograph in the George Grantham Bain Collection, 1912. *Library of Congress Prints and Photographs Division.*

Some feared he was an "outlaw Tarzan," according to the *Adirondack Record-Elizabethtown Post.* The mere sight of the man startled the two trappers, who said they felt threatened by the "shotgun-armed wanderer," according to the *Chateaugay Record.* He had done no harm to them or to their property, but his appearance was frightful, they said, with his hulking size and ragged clothing. So they reported their brief encounter to the sheriff of Long Lake, who notified the state police. With that, the man's fate was sealed. Nobody knew if he was an escaped convict or fugitive from justice (for which there might be a reward), a lunatic, a hermit or a real live wild man. They had no idea if he was guilty of a crime or not. And they never would, because he took his identity to the grave the day they hunted him down and shot him.

The posse of troopers was led by Lieutenant C.B. McCann of the New York State Police barracks in Malone. He had hoped to apprehend the man without a fight, but it wasn't to be. For three days, they tracked the man some twenty miles through the rugged, snow-covered wilderness, and somehow—even without shoes—the scantily clad mountain man outpaced the search party, whose members were dressed appropriately for the job.

Photograph by Bernard Moses. *Library of Congress Prints and Photographs Division.*

They found the man at an abandoned lumber camp in the dense woods between Newcomb and Long Lake. It appeared, by the packed snow cover, that he had been using the camp for shelter for quite some time. McCann called out to the man, who was hiding in the cabin, to surrender. The response was a shotgun blast from within, resulting in return fire that struck the trapped man in the leg. The man then climbed out a back window, according to several accounts, and hobbled off into the woods, carrying one of his two old shotguns. It didn't take long before he was again surrounded, just inside the Essex County line, where he had taken cover behind a mound of snow. Again, he was urged to surrender peacefully as a trooper and a game warden approached him, and again he responded with gunfire. Only this time, the posse's return fire dropped him where he knelt in the snow. Before they could determine his identity, his eyes rolled back in his head and he was gone.

On closer inspection—now that they had him—the Wild Man of the Adirondacks appeared to be in his mid-thirties. He was enormous in build and looked about as scruffy as one might expect of someone living in the wild. The tattered rags he wore for clothing suggested that he had been living in the wild for some time. He had no clothing appropriate for the harsh climate—no shoes, gloves, hats or outerwear—but his hands were carefully wrapped with rags and his feet and legs with fresh deer hide for warmth. For this reason, it was felt that he had subsisted primarily on deer meat for God knows how long. In his pocket was a wad of several old dollar bills no longer in circulation, as well as a single newer dollar bill, indicating that he had, on at least one recent occasion, ventured out of the safety of the deep woods and into society—a move that would seal his fate. One news article suggested that perhaps he simply needed to purchase ammunition with which to hunt.

The snow was too deep to carry the body out of the woods without a sled, so it was left there overnight. Officers returned the next day to retrieve it and deliver it to Indian Lake. Because the man carried no identification and nobody seemed to recognize him, fingerprints were taken by Coroner Gaus of Ticonderoga during the inquest to see if perhaps he was an escaped convict, and the man's description was broadly publicized in an effort to find someone who knew who he was. No match to the fingerprints was found, and nobody knew who he was. Looking back, people in the vicinity recalled having seen, over the years, campfires left smoldering in the wilderness, crude shacks here and there that nobody held claim to, glimpses of skulking bigfoot-like figures in the woods and so on. These were all things that might have been attributed to the Wild Man of the Adirondacks. It appears he had lived for years in the wild, never bothering a soul, until the day they came for him.

Twenty years later, another "weird, half-naked" wild man was spotted near Lost Pond in Essex County, and a reporter for the *Ticonderoga Sentinel* quipped that perhaps a "mysterious wanderer" in the vast wilderness of that region should be an "object of envy" rather than pity because he had chosen to remove himself from the distractions of modern technology and the obligations of society. The article further stated that perhaps those who felt sorry for the wild man had things backwards in considering him a "demented creature" and that maybe *he* thought we were the demented ones for choosing to function as we do in this "wacky, woozy world."

Hip to Be Hobo

Clinton County, 1880–1925

Beggar, vagrant, hobo, bum—call them what you will, but in the late 1800s and early 1900s, the people to whom such dated terms applied were mostly called tramps in Northern New York. Of course, today, the politically correct term would be "homeless person," and they are treated with much more compassion and dignity, and have greater resources available to them, than back then. But yesteryear's homeless were good at improvising to compensate for lack of resources. They didn't object to using jailhouses as a suitable lodging option, for example, or bumming a good meal off a kindhearted sheriff. The *Plattsburgh Sentinel* of December 3, 1909, ran an article stating that Sheriff Nash had provided the prisoners of the Clinton County jail with "an excellent Thanksgiving dinner." The article added that more than a third of the jail population consisted of tramps:

> *The caring for prisoners in the county jail is no small task. From January 1, 1909, up to yesterday morning, 641 persons had the keys turned on them. Of this number, 228 were tramps either committed under charge, or who had applied for lodging.*

So the homeless simply "applied for lodging," unless they had allegedly committed a crime. And while they did commit their share of robberies in the area, there were times when they were blamed and carted off to jail just because they looked the part of the villain. In December 1878, the *Sentinel* reported on a burglary at the Day Store in Peru. One morning when the clerk arrived to open up, he found that the place had been robbed. Someone had climbed up on a barrel, smashed in the rear window, reached over the broken glass to raise the bar that secured the door and let himself in. Once inside, he closed the shades on the other windows and lit a lamp before helping himself to the merchandise. He broke open a money drawer containing about ten dollars ($222 today). He also made off with "several fine razors, five pairs of overshoes, a pair of rubber boots, a quantity of tobacco, and numerous toilet articles, such as cologne, soap, hair oil, tooth powders, etc." The article quipped, "They were evidently high-toned, first-class tramps!"

Created by Shober & Carqueville, Chicago, circa 1890. *Library of Congress Prints and Photographs Division.*

Five tramps had been seen in Peru the day before the burglary, during which five pairs of overshoes, five bottles of cologne and five bars of soap were stolen. The coincidence was not lost on authorities, who quickly located the men at the St. Louis House, thought they fit the bill and arrested them on the spot. The search for the thieves was then called off. The *Sentinel* said:

> *Monday afternoon Mr. Day came to Plattsburgh…and visited the jail, identifying the tramps without doubt as the men who were seen in Peru Sunday morning, one of whom begged a breakfast of Mr. Day. But to his surprise, the tramps were able easily to prove an alibi, as Mr. St. Louis affirmed that they came to his hotel Sunday afternoon and remained at his house overnight, while Mr. Day is positive that the burglary was committed after ten o'clock Sunday night, as he was in the store just before ten, and examined the drawer and some of the very goods that were missed the next morning. The prisoners were, of course, set at liberty. And yet the circumstantial evidence is of the strongest kind…Five tramps were seen to enter Plattsburgh Sunday afternoon, on the*

Peru road. Five tramps put up that night at the hotel named, and it seems hard to resist the conviction that somehow they were connected with the burglary.

The obvious questions are, did the men look spiffy and were they wearing new shoes when they were arrested? Did they even have any of the missing items in their possession? Apparently not, or they would have been detained. Instead, they were released, and the real culprits—tramps or otherwise—got away.

The trio who burglarized the Holcombe & Bruso store in Rouses Point in 1909 wasn't so lucky. They forced three doors open before going "about their work deliberately, selecting clothing with great care and taking the best stock," according to the *Sentinel*. They made off with jewelry and apparel valued at $3,650 in today's dollars, which is a pretty impressive heist, but these guys were not the sharpest tools in the shed. According to the December 9, 1909 issue of the *Plattsburgh Sentinel*:

The thieves changed their clothes in the store, leaving their old rags behind, and it was by these rags that it became known that the burglary was the work of the tramps seen in the village early in the evening and also at Alburgh

Photograph by the Brown Brothers, 1905. *Library of Congress Prints and Photographs Division.*

> [Vermont], *as persons who had seen the hobos positively identified the clothes left in the store as those worn by the tramps.*

A search was quickly made for the homeless men in question, and they were found at Lacolle, Quebec, just eight miles away, where they were waiting for a westbound train. The article closed by saying, "This is the third time within the past five years that this store has been burglarized, and each time it has undoubtedly been the work of tramps." But the problem with the homeless population wasn't just its contribution to crime; they also contributed to typhus, according to New York State in 1881, when it issued the following notice published in the *Plattsburgh Republican* on November 12:

> *Warning against Typhus—The typhus contagion which is being spread by tramps and vagrants, threatens much harm. Each of the 20 cities beyond the metropolis* [New York City], *and local boards of health in the 331 villages and 933 towns of the State, should require their Health Officers to be watchful and ready to adopt all necessary sanitary precautions for isolating and controlling this disease at its first appearance.*
>
> *Tramps should not be permitted to enter dwellings and lodging houses, as they wander from the cities. They should be cleansed and directed by the Superintendent of the Poor.*

Published by the Baine News Service. *Library of Congress Prints and Photographs Division.*

They had become a threat, not just to a man's wallet, but also to his health, and there seemed to be nothing Clinton County could do to stop them. In 1886, the *Sentinel* noted the undeniable presence of homeless vagabonds, saying, "Tramps are reported as being very numerous along the line of the O&LC Railroad between Ogdensburg and Rouses Point." Twenty years later, there was even a resort for tramps passing through the Plattsburgh area that was dubbed the Rouses Point Canteen. The *Republican* explained in its August 10, 1907 paper:

> *It is an encampment on a knoll about a mile west of* [Rouses Point] *between the Rutland railroad and the Canadian border. It is frequented by tramps who come and go, staying awhile as at a hotel and then moving on. Here, they sleep in the open, cooking and eating such food as they can beg, borrow or steal. This knoll affords a lookout, and they keep a close watch for strangers. The "guests" at the resort seem to be a harmless set of hoboes. It seems to be widely known in the tramp fraternity and to be the objective point for long journeys and a place for exchange of ideas and plans.*

Plattsburgh Chief of Police Connors learned about the camp after a homeless man who had been arrested promised to "clear out and make that his destination." That was when Connors, Detective Libby and Inspector Yale (of the Immigration Service) visited the Rouses Point Canteen to see if a fugitive from justice who was wanted in another city might have found his way to the tramp camp at Rouses Point. They didn't find the man they wanted, but they did learn about a similar setup just across the border in Canada, between Rouses Point and Lacolle, Quebec. They were a problem everywhere.

Finally, in 1925, someone in authority took a bold stand against the tramp population in Clinton County. Plattsburgh city judge J. Edgar Downs publicly warned all tramps to "steer clear of Plattsburgh," saying, "The impression seems to prevail among the [tramp] fraternity that Plattsburgh is an easy place…I want to dispel that impression." He then asked a "state tramp" named John Lynch, who was being sentenced that day, if "he wanted to be sworn and give his reasons for being in this part of the country without visible means of support." Without missing a beat, the witty man replied, "No. I don't swear." Emmett Kelly, the creator of the most famous hobo of all—a Depression-era clown called Weary Willie—would be proud. He made it hip to be hobo.

The Man Who Stole a Hundred Horses

Franklin County, 1890–1906

In the nineteenth century, North Country residents depended on their horses for both their livelihood (i.e. farming) and their primary means of transportation. To find oneself robbed of one's horse was no trivial matter. Indeed, many early horse thieves were hanged for their crimes. Horse thieves walked into one town or settlement searching for a suitable target, walked off into the night with a stolen horse or two and headed to the next town or county, where they could sell or trade without suspicion. Before the invention of the automobile, it was a big problem, and it could carry a heavy penalty—a price some weren't willing to pay.

On June 11, 1923, for example, an elderly Clinton County man named Nelson Duvarney rented a horse and rig from a stable in Burlington, Vermont (across Lake Champlain) with no intention of ever returning it. That's one way to steal a horse. But this wasn't his first rodeo; he had been captured two years earlier with a stolen horse and rig at Ellenburg. When he didn't return to the Burlington stable after several days, Burlington police sent Plattsburgh and other nearby police agencies a description of Duvarney and the stolen horse and rig, and Clinton County Sheriff Day forwarded the description to his deputies. On June 30, forty miles north of Plattsburgh, in Sainte-Clotilde-de-Châteauguay, Quebec, Duvarney was apprehended by Deputy Sheriff William Stevenson of Mooers, who sent word to Day that he was returning with the eighty-year-old prisoner to Plattsburgh. Duvarney, however, became ill during the short journey, and his condition declined rapidly as the party approached Plattsburgh. Dr. Clough came at once to examine the prisoner, but Duvarney died forty-five minutes later. A half-filled bottle of acid was found in his pocket, and it was determined that he had purchased it in Canada to ingest if he was caught rather than face a long prison sentence in Vermont.

Other horse thieves didn't take themselves so seriously. Charles White had just been released from jail after serving twenty days for horse stealing when he stole another horse and light harness from the barn of William McKinney on Cornelia Street in Plattsburgh on the night of December 30, 1910. The theft was thankfully discovered quickly, and the police were notified and began following White's tracks through the snow. About two or three hours later, Sheriff Nash apprehended the man near Salmon River, where he was

Photograph taken by Pinkerton's National Detective Agency, circa 1900. *Library of Congress Prints and Photographs Division.*

still guiding the stolen horse through the darkness. The horse was returned to its owners, and White was locked up again. Yet Charlie White's arrests seemed like child's play compared to Lon Clark's brushes with the law.

Alonzo "Lon" Clark was a star among outlaws in the late 1800s, with his name and career of choice (horse thief) in headlines often—usually preceded by adjectives like noted, notorious and celebrated. Had his photograph ever accompanied the many articles—so people would know whom to beware of—he might not have gotten away with it quite so often. J.D. Sullivan of Canton didn't recognize the famous thief when a man calling himself Harry Nash hired a horse and buggy from Sullivan's livery and sales stables in 1893. When "Nash" didn't return at the agreed-upon time and three days had passed, Sullivan had no choice but to track him down. Nash had told him he was going to Hewittville, so that's the first place Sullivan checked. There, he found some of his buggy gear, and he learned that Nash had attempted to trade the horse. But an alert would-be buyer named McLellan, whom Nash was told to meet in Norwood, sensed that something wasn't right with the transaction and refused to buy the horse. In fact, he went so far as to threaten to have the horse thief arrested. Knowing his plan was foiled, Nash (aka Clark) made haste to Knapps Station to put up for the night. The next morning, he snuck out without the horse and buggy; they were locked up in separate barns, and to try and get either one of them would be too time-consuming and risky, considering the circumstances. He knew he hadn't a moment to spare. The *Adirondack News* of October 28, 1893, said:

> *Mr. Sullivan secured his property Monday and learned that Nash is the famous horse thief, Lon Clark, who ended a term in states prison, June 17th, having served four years and over for the Colton robbery, when he went off with liveryman Quin's rig. It was only a short time ago that he stole a horse in Hogansburg, and one in Malone. Three warrants are now out for his arrest.*

Clark thrived on such media accounts—and there were many. The *Malone Gazette*, with its usual wit, said later that week, "If our St. Lawrence county exchanges are correct in their statements, the celebrated Lon Clark has again resumed his profession of appropriating other people's horses." That's a kinder, gentler way of putting it. Clark was riding under the radar for five months before his capture near Whippleville in March 1894, when he was again arrested. The *Malone Palladium* of March 22, 1894, said:

> *Under Sheriff Ketchum and Constable Boyea succeeded in apprehending the notorious horse thief, "Lon" Clark, on Saturday last…The offense for which Clark is to answer is the theft of a horse from Mr. Bero, of Hogansburgh* [sic], *last fall. He was indicted last week. Clark was discharged from Dannemora last summer and is said to have since stolen horses at Canton and Bangor, besides the one at Hogansburgh. Only a few days before the latter theft, he told an acquaintance in Dickinson that his record up to that date was ninety-nine horses stolen, and that one more was needed to bring it up to a round hundred. It seems the one lacking was supplied, and for it, he is likely to again go to prison, where a good part of his life has been passed. Clark strenuously denies that he is guilty.*

Of course he did. How else was he to maintain his title (of world's greatest horse thief) if jail time kept interrupting his criminal pursuits? He had been in jail for just over three months when he was released in June 1894, and he walked out of the courtroom wearing a coat and vest he had "borrowed" from a fellow prisoner so he would look respectable in court. But the prisoner insisted it was stolen. For *that* offense, Clark was captured a few days later and committed to jail for *another* four months. When his time in the Franklin County jail expired in mid-October 1894, he was turned over to St. Lawrence County authorities, and Sullivan (whose horse and buggy had been taken by Clark the previous October) identified him as the man who had done him wrong. That case went to the grand jury. In March 1895, Judge Swift sentenced Clark to "five years at Dannemora," according to the *Gazette*, which added (with a yawn), "It was the same old charge—horse stealing."

Three and a half years later, Lon Clark was released from prison for the umpteenth time, swearing he had turned over a new leaf. The *Gazette* had once referred to Clark as "the notorious horse thief…whose criminal history would fill a book." Clark took the hint and ran with it. In December 1898, he decided to leave his life of crime behind and concentrate, instead, on writing his autobiography. The *Malone Palladium* of December 22, 1898, said:

> *Alonzo Clark, the famous horse thief, was in Malone last week, negotiating for the publication of a book of his life and crimes, which he has nearly completed in manuscript form. His history is an interesting one, and if the book ever makes its appearance, it will doubtless meet with ready sale. He says he can sell 5,000 copies in this county. During his life of crime, he has served 17 years in prison, and his last sentence was completed only*

> *four months ago, when he was released from Dannemora. His home is in Dickinson Center, where he now resides.*
>
> *He says that he is a reformed horse thief and will never take up the profession again. He made it his life work and is content to let the record stand, which he thinks makes him the champion living horse thief of the United States. When asked by the writer how many States he had operated in, he replied, "From the Atlantic to the Pacific coast," and he added that 350 horses would not cover the total number stolen. He has a complete list of the horses, giving places, dates, etc. His one regret seems to be that he did not get rich out of the work, considering the risk attached to it, but he says that in his 40 years of horse stealing, he never heard of but two thieves who saved any money. As a rule, they live well as long as they have money, and then resort to their profession again.*
>
> *Clark informs us that the first thing he ever stole was a goose egg from Asa Harwood's father, who lived in Dickinson Center…Clark seems to have had a mania for stealing horses, and he says he never cared to steal anything else. He is a well preserved man of about 60 years, and it seems likely that his reformation is sincere and permanent.*

Indeed, it was. For the next five and a half years, Clark stayed true to his word and remained clean. If his book was ever published, it must have been an incredible read. In June 1906, Lon Clark passed away at his home in Dickinson. The *Adirondack News* said:

> *Notwithstanding his horse record, Clark had many good qualities and was by no means as bad as those who did not know him would think. So far as we have been able to learn, his last years were those of a quiet, law-abiding citizen.*

And the *Malone Palladium* summed up the thoughts of many with a memorable, lighthearted quip, saying, "The horse world will rest easier now that [Clark] has departed to other fields."

The Tarring and Feathering of Mrs. Covey

Jayville/Fine, 1895

It is something for the whole country to hide its head in shame over—that mob of men who stripped a woman's clothes off her and held her while a mob of women in men's clothes and with blackened faces applied tar and feathers to her naked body.
—Courier & Freeman, *August 14, 1895*

In mid-May 1895, John Kirch of Jayville left his wife and four children, as well as a good job as a superintendent at the *Post & Henderson* that paid $1,200 per year. His boss, W.J. Henderson, said Kirch was a "highly honorable man" whom he trusted implicitly. Imagine everyone's surprise, then, when it came to light that Kirch had withdrawn all the money he had in the bank and made off with the deed to his property and his pension papers, leaving his wife and children with absolutely nothing. A quiet investigation showed that Mrs. Bert (Hattie) Covey, the young wife of a section hand on the Camden and Amboy Railroad (C&A), who had formerly lived at Jayville, also disappeared at the same time—and the two paramours allegedly departed on the same train together, bound for Ohio. The *St. Lawrence Republican*, in describing Hattie Covey, said:

> *She is a slender woman weighing less than a hundred pounds, and is about twenty-two years of age. She is of French Canadian descent, rather good-looking, but ignorant, being unable to read or write. She was formerly Hattie Nervin, and her parents who are industrious and thrifty*

Courtesy of the author.

> *people, lived in Ogdensburg until sixteen years ago. Their children, Hattie included, were born here.*

The *Watertown Re-Union* of May 29, 1895, said, "Common report has it that [Hattie Covey and John Kirch] have been unduly intimate for some time past." The *Watertown Herald* said that Bert Covey had moved with Hattie away from Jayville to Carthage some time before because of the "marked attention Kirch paid to his wife." The move did nothing to extinguish the forbidden romance, for the wayward lovers continued to correspond and meet in secret. If anything, it made them more determined to be together.

Henderson echoed the sentiments of the Jayville community when he said, "Queer thing [is], Kirch has thrown away his position, his prospects, and left his family, besides ruining forever Covey's family in pursuit of a guilty love." At the time, nobody could have foreseen what would transpire two months later, as a result of the unholy union—an event that would thrust St. Lawrence County into the national spotlight and earn Jayville a seat of prominence in the hall of shame. Mrs. Kirch was a woman scorned. For two months, night after lonely night, day after unbearable day, Laura Kirch could think only of her disdain for Hattie Covey, whom she blamed for destroying her family and bringing shame on the family name. She decided that, if the woman her husband ran off with ever stepped foot in town again, she would make sure that she knew what it felt like to be publicly humiliated.

She didn't have to wait long. Hattie returned from Ohio in late July, arriving in Carthage en route to her parents' home in Jayville, a hamlet in the town of Fine. As fate would have it, Laura Kirch happened to be aboard the same coach and had secured a seat at the opposite end of the train from Hattie. Hence, she knew that her nemesis had returned, and it was time to call in backup.

Hattie, who was unaware that Laura was onboard, got off the train and went straight to stay with her mother, Mrs. Julia Nevin, who kept a boardinghouse in the community. Late that evening, two men showed up at the door warning Hattie that she would be tarred and feathered—and her mother's house would be torn down—if she didn't leave town immediately. Tarring and feathering is a barbaric, antiquated type of civilian retribution. But in the distant past, it was a form of vigilante justice occasionally meted out on someone who had done somebody wrong. The person was held down and stripped at least to the waist, and hot tar was then either painted or poured on the victim's bare skin just prior to covering him or her with feathers. Victims were often then publicly displayed, because the ultimate goal of tarring and feathering was to humiliate an individual and send an unmistakable message.

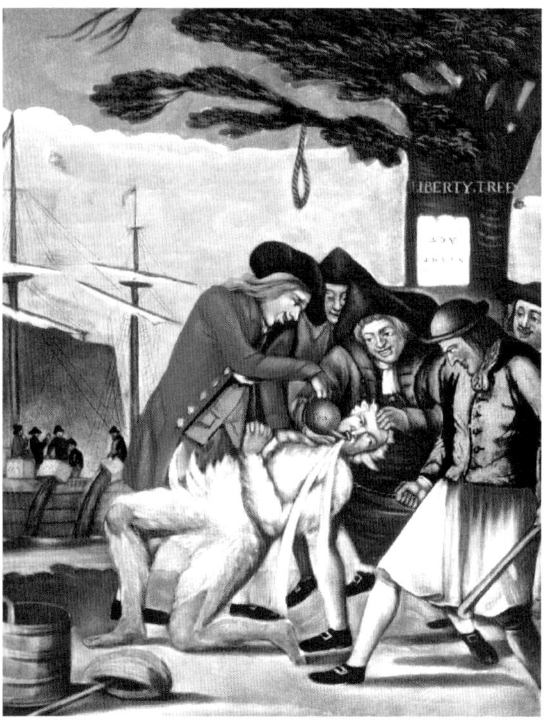

Created by Robert Sayer and John Bennett, 1774. *Library of Congress Prints and Photographs Division.*

Refusing to be intimidated, Hattie and her mother and two brothers went to Pitcairn the next day and "swore out a warrant for the arrest of the two men who had called on her."

The family then boarded the evening train at Bacon's Crossing to return home. The *Daily Journal* of July 31, 1895, describes what happened next:

> *When the train stopped at the station, the mother and daughter got off of the rear platform and walked to the front of the train, where they were suddenly surrounded by a crowd of men who seized the daughter and took her into the railroad freight house, where they stripped her. There was a crowd of women there, dressed in men's clothes and with blackened faces. The men held the woman down on the floor, while the women applied the tar and feathers with a paint brush, completely covering her with the stuff, after which they left her. She was taken to her mother's house, where a physician was called. It was found that one arm and a number of ribs were broken. It is said to be doubtful if she lives. Her husband was informed of the affair, but has not gone to Jayville as yet.*

No doubt, he was afraid that the same fate would await him. It was later determined that Hattie's arms and ribs were not broken, as originally believed, but that she was considerably bruised from her ordeal. Besides the tarring and feathering, her attackers took her purse, which contained $10.20, along with her hat and gloves. Her attorney said he would have the perpetrators arrested and charged with first-degree robbery, punishable by up to twenty years in jail. The story was so sensational that it was even reported in the *New York Times* on July 31, 1895, in an article called "Woman Tarred and Feathered," which said, "Jayville, a village on the fringe of the Adirondack forest, above Carthage, has been the scene of the punishment of a woman, in a manner which has outraged decency." Such was the thought among all law-abiding citizens. The case was dubbed the "Jayville Outrage."

It didn't take long to have the key players in the mob that attacked Hattie Covey arrested, for they were all easily recognized and well known, even those going incognito. The examination before Justice of the Peace Shipman of Pitcairn lasted three days and resulted in five people being held to await the action of the grand jury on charges of riot and assault. Besides Laura Kirch, the others included her son, Charles; Eugene Olen; George Clark, the station agent at Jayville and son-in-law of the Kirches; and Stein Ferguson. District Attorney Hale of St. Lawrence County was secured to appear for the people, along with Assistant District Attorney George W. Hurlbut of Heuvelton, while H.J. Welch of Carthage had the task of representing the defendants. Testimony taken during the examination indicated that Laura

Kirch, Eugene Olen and Charles Kirch wore masks, and they "were the only ones that laid violent hands upon the woman," according to the *St. Lawrence Republican* of August 14, 1895:

> *Ferguson and Clark were not masked but aided and abetted the crime by keeping the woman's friends from assisting her to escape, and Clark furnished the place where the woman was tarred and feathered, and blew out the lights. There were also a large crowd of men present, who closed about the woman when she was seized by her assailants and thus assisted in preventing her friends from getting near to assist her.*
>
> *She was accompanied by her mother and two brothers, and when she descended from the car, she was seized upon by those in disguise and a struggle ensued between them and her friends. One of her brothers was knocked down and the other crowded to the outside of the circle of men around his sister. He drew a revolver and made a rush at the crowd, swearing that he would release her. It was here that Ferguson interfered. He threw his arm around the boy from behind, carried him around behind the station, took the revolver away from him, and held him there.*
>
> *Her mother was the last one to let Mrs. Covey go. She is a heavy woman and hung to her daughter by the waist until the steps leading into the freight shed were reached, when her hold was loosened, and the unfortunate woman was dragged within and the door closed. She was thrown upon the floor of the freight shed and testifies that Charles Kirch had her by the throat and that Mrs. Kirch called out, "For God's sake, Charlie, don't kill her," whereupon he loosed his hold on her throat and placed his knee on her chest. Then they tore the clothing from the upper portion of her body and daubed it, as well as her head and face, with tar and feathers. They then treated the lower portion of her body in the same manner and thrust her into the open air through an outhouse at the rear of the freight shed.*

At the close of the examination, with the accused parties offering no defense, Laura Kirch, the ringleader, was discharged to await grand jury action, and the four men involved were released on $200 bail. In October 1895, all five of the accused were indicted by the grand jury and pleaded guilty to the charge of "unlawful assemblage." Laura was fined $50; her son Charles and Stein Ferguson were fined $75 each; and George Clark and Eugene Olen were each fined $150 (roughly $4,000 in today's dollars). All of them paid their fines, and that was the end of that ugly incident in North Country history—but another tarring and feathering almost occurred several years later.

In 1902, there was a near-fatal shooting that began with a plan to tar and feather an individual named William Prue in Westville Center in Franklin County. In that case, according to the *Fort Covington Sun*, an angry mob surrounded the house of the sixty-year-old Prue with "the avowed intention of tarring and feathering" him. Stories had been circulating around his community to the effect that Prue "had deserted his wife and that the housekeeper still remained," suggesting that he left his wife for his housekeeper, Mrs. Desaw. Even though he adamantly denied the gossip, some of his neighbors were determined to disgrace him, so they gathered around his house, armed with guns and rocks one night, hollering for him to come out and face the consequences of his alleged actions. Shots were fired into the windows, and Prue was struck in both the chest and the neck. When the mob members realized that they might have killed the man they had intended only to tar and feather, they quickly dispersed before authorities could reach the scene. When Sheriff Douglass, District Attorney Gordon H. Main and Dr. R.J. Wilding arrived on the scene, they found the man in critical condition. Every window in his home had been shattered in the mêlée, and large stones were scattered across the floor inside. The sheriff vowed that "wholesale arrests [were] threatened." Prue survived (only to commit suicide seventeen years later), but no arrests were ever made, from what I can tell, and no leader of the mob that wanted to tar and feather him over unsubstantiated rumors was ever identified.

The *Courier & Freeman* summed up the act of tarring and feathering well in a scathing column regarding the Covey case on August 14, 1895, which said:

> *How much of the recklessness and rude justice or injustice of pioneer times still lurks in the oldest and most civilized states of this Union has been demonstrated by the tarring and feathering of a woman in the Adirondack region in New York…Such a scene could not have been witnessed among the most lawless cowboys of the western ranges. No! It was left for a community in the Empire State to disgrace the American republic in that way. It is to be hoped that there is law enough in the Empire State to punish the perpetrators of the shameful outrage. We claim to be a civilized Christian people. Whatever offense against morality and good order is committed, there are always legal methods of reaching the transgressor.*

Incredibly, in the case of Hattie Covey, the punishment of the mob that attacked her consisted of nothing more than a mere fine for each individual involved. Apparently, there wasn't "law enough" to punish the perpetrators more than that.

The Taking (and Return... Seventeen Years Later) of Little Freddie Brosseau

Sissonville/Potsdam, 1896

On October 21, 1896, six-year-old Freddie Brosseau vanished. He was last seen shortly before 6:00 p.m., playing on a bridge between his Sissonville home and the A. Sherman Lumber Company mill where his father worked. The boy sometimes walked alone the short distance to meet his father in the late afternoon, but that day, when he didn't show up at the mill or at his home, his parents, John and Celia Brosseau, began a frantic search for him. Soon, the searching party consisted of nearly all available hands in the close-knit community. The *Northern Tribune* said, "The mill was shut down, the flumes emptied and all carefully searched. The river banks and surrounding country were scoured, and the river bed raked, but the little form could not be found."

The *Ogdensburg Daily Journal* of October 30, 1896, said:

> *He had been playing with several other little boys; and, as he stood by the mill, a workman came out, patted him on the head and asked if he was waiting for his father. Where he went from there is still a mystery. Not coming home, his parents grew alarmed and the search commenced. It has been kept up ever since, but without finding a trace of the little fellow... Over near the farther end of the bridge* [he had been playing at] *was a little hole covered by some wagons. It was not large enough for a man to go through, but a small boy might. The children had been playing hide and seek and possibly Freddie went in there, fell on the rocks below and was carried down river by the swift waters.*

Photograph in the Frances Benjamin Johnston Collection, 1888. *Library of Congress Prints and Photographs Division.*

The only other possibility was that two "rough-appearing strangers" who were loitering near the mill that day had something to do with the boy's disappearance. But they were never seen again. I wonder if the wagons covering that little hole were those of gypsies passing through the area and if the two unknown men were part of the caravan. Years later, an incredible story of kidnap would emerge—starring none other than Freddie Brosseau and a band of lawless gypsies. But as fall turned to winter in 1896, the most common theory was that the child had "drowned and his body [was] lodged somewhere on the river bottom." You can imagine the family's heartbreak when days turned to weeks, then to months and then years, and they were no closer than they had been that fateful afternoon in determining what had become of their child. Yet, they never gave up hope that he would one day return to them.

Fast-forward seventeen years. According to the *Courier & Freeman* of August 20, 1913:

> *Two weeks ago last Monday, a young man applied for aid to a Catholic Father on a boat on the Ottawa River. He had escaped from gypsies, he said, and had a tale to tell of cruelty and ill treatment, inhuman and well-*

> *nigh past belief. He could recall that he came from northern New York and that his name was Frederick. He knew he had been stolen, for his captors had beaten him unmercifully whenever he spoke of his former home. The father was impressed with the story and took the young man to the Trappist Monastery at Oka.*

While the Trappist monks are generally men of few words, their young visitor had plenty to say to them and to anyone who would listen. He didn't know his birthday, but he looked to be about twenty-three or twenty-four years of age. He remembered being called Frederick as a youth, but the gypsies gave him the name "Patrick" and had "beaten him up and ill-used him whenever he attempted to assert that he did not rightly belong with them," according to the *Massena Observer*. In an effort to determine exactly who this young man with such a mysterious past was, the information he provided to the monks was shared with the news media in the Montreal area. And the monks then contacted Father Marron of St. Mary's in Potsdam because Marron was their friend and their Northern New York liaison. If anyone could help them find out about missing children, he could. At the same time, newspapers in the Montreal metropolitan area were carrying young Brosseau's story, along with photographs of him. And as fate would have it, Mrs. Brosseau's sister, Kate Perry, lived in Montreal and saw the articles. She paid a visit to the monastery to see if the photograph she had of Freddie that was taken shortly before he went missing resembled the young man at Oka.

The *Norwood News* said, "A comparison between the unknown and unidentified boy and the picture were quickly made, and the result was that she was satisfied in her own mind that the lad who had made such a fight to escape the clutches of the gypsies was no other than her nephew." What's more, he vaguely remembered posing for that photograph at some type of memorial occasion! Mrs. Perry then contacted the couple in Potsdam to give Celia and John the incredible news. Accompanied by another of their eight children, son Frank (then a lawyer in Potsdam), and Father Marron, the Brosseaus headed to Montreal and to the monastery at Oka in hopes of confirming the identity of their son.

When they arrived at the monastery, the parents were able to "pick their son out of a crowd in the courtyard," according to the *Courier & Freeman*, "and by a birthmark on the right arm and a slight blemish on the forehead." Their son had a very distinctive birthmark on his arm, which the gypsies had attempted to burn off with acid, and the young man bore a striking resemblance to the family, especially to his brother Frank. The two could have passed as twins. The icing on the cake was when he told his family that a female gypsy who cared for him for years, acting as a nanny of sorts, had passed away three years earlier. On her deathbed, she called him to her side and told him he had been stolen from Potsdam, New York, "where gypsies stayed the day he was kidnapped," according to the *Norwood News*. The Brousseaus were now certain that this person was their long-lost son and were shocked to hear of all he had been through while in captivity. The *Courier* said:

> *The story of Brosseau's wanderings since he was stolen seventeen years ago is a remarkable one. In this time, he was taken through four foreign countries, Spain, France, Italy, and Bohemia, remaining long enough in each to learn to speak the language fluently. His first journey abroad was thirteen years ago. Since that time, the band has spent each winter in foreign lands.*
>
> *The caravan in which he found himself made a practice of stealing children at every opportunity, the girls being invariably sold for money. Young Brosseau, stealing up behind the head men of the tribe one night, saw $500 in cash paid for one young girl. There were, up to a short time ago, three kidnapped children with the band, including Brosseau. He aided a young boy to escape several weeks ago. The other child, a girl, is still with them. The Canadian police are hot on their trail, however, and hope to overhaul them soon.*
>
> *Brosseau's story of the tortures to which he and his companions were subjected dims those of the ancient savages and beggars description. Beaten with poisoned whips, their bodies dipped in poisonous oil to make the flesh swell, pounded with clubs until their backs were a mass of bruises, it is remarkable that the captives survived.*

In light of the information regarding the gypsy kidnappers provided by young Brosseau, Montreal police had no choice but to detain him as a witness, necessarily restricting him to the monastery grounds about forty miles from Montreal, and they told him it would probably be three or four weeks, at least, that he would have to remain there. If they captured the kidnappers, the trial would last at least that long. So his family bade him a bittersweet farewell, fully expecting to be reunited soon enough. The *Norwood News* said:

> *The feelings of the anxious father and mother, the joy of the long lost boy and son, and the tender words that passed between the members of the united family have no place here. After years of careful and continued*

> *search, the parents have found their son, and after years of cruelty from his captors and beatings and kicks from those who kept him in their power, the son has found a loving and kind mother and father awaiting his return there.*

That was August 15, 1918. Unfortunately, with all the publicity the story had generated, the gypsies knew they would find "Patrick" at Oka, and they "did all in their power to get the young man back to them," but the monks succeeded, for a time, in foiling their plans, even having two of the gypsies arrested (although, they quickly escaped the police). Hell hath no fury like a band of gypsies scorned. On Friday, September 6, less than three weeks after the Brosseaus had finally found their son, they were given the shocking news that he had disappeared—again, and this time it was for good. The *Norwood News* described the bizarre turn of events:

> *The circumstances surrounding the young man's disappearance are unusual and several stories are being circulated in the Canadian metropolis regarding it. The last seen of "Patrick" was at the monastery shortly before the time set for his baptism and confirmation, which was to have taken place on August 22.*
>
> *The young man was seen conversing with a stranger in the court yard and seemed anxious and perturbed. A few moments later, he was nowhere to be seen, and as time wore on and he did not appear, a search about the grounds was instituted for him, but without result. It is believed at Oka that he has again been stolen. It is also rumored there that he was seen at the Place Visger station in Montreal taking a New York train, in company with a woman who claimed to be his mother.*

It is presumed that his gypsy "family" convinced him, probably with threats, to return to their clan, and after that, who knows what became of him? Nobody ever heard from him again, so the Freddie Brosseau mystery was never solved. And three years after the seemingly miraculous, though short-lived, reunion that left many people with more questions than answers, his heartbroken mother, Celia Brosseau, passed away, following a long and painful battle with cancer. The *Courier & Freeman* of August 30, 1916, said in its obituary for Mrs. Brosseau that Freddie had "disappeared again as mysteriously as before, and the father and mother gave up hope again."

Beware of Brothels (and Maidens with Blond Tresses)

Northern New York, Early 1900s

Steen Ferguson has been granted an absolute divorce from his wife. She was proven to be a woman of ill repute, and the incidents recited of her callousness were shameful. Steen is a farmer, and will hereafter stick to the "good old plan" and fight shy of the maidens with blonde tresses.
—Watertown Herald, *November 13, 1897*

If you thought people were modest prudes in the Victorian and Edwardian eras, let me assure you that they were far from it. Never in the history of Northern New York were there more houses of ill fame, and women of ill repute, than in the late 1800s and early 1900s. The *Plattsburgh Sentinel* of March 17, 1881, implored the public to do something about it, asking, "Is there not enterprise and ingenuity enough among our Plattsburgh citizens to devise some way to close up the numberless houses of ill-repute that infest our village? Some of them are said to be on our most public streets."

Plattsburgh wasn't alone. In St. Lawrence County, the Pine Grove district of Massena, for example, had "several houses of ill repute [that] were being run full blast" in 1923, according to the *Ogdensburg Republican-Journal.* On April 30 of that year, Chief of Police B.J. Demo orchestrated a raid and sent several officers to the area where the houses were located. Because the local jail was too crowded with the resultant arrests, Judge Giles Chase held a special hearing on a Sunday morning to lighten the burden. One woman charged with keeping a house of ill repute and renting out rooms for "immoral purposes" pled guilty and was offered three months in jail with a fifty-dollar

Courtesy of the author.

fine, *or* she could leave Massena on the afternoon train, which she gladly promised to do. A Syracuse woman arrested in Massena for prostitution pleaded guilty. She was fined fifty dollars and sentenced to three months in jail, unless she agreed to leave town immediately after paying the fine. A third woman charged with prostitution pleaded guilty and was fined fifty dollars and sentenced to three months in jail. She, too, could avoid jail time by agreeing to "leave town and never return."

Two local men were caught with their pants down in the raid, figuratively speaking, but they were let off easy. After using them as witnesses against several houses with which the men were intimately familiar, Judge Chase only lectured them on amending their ways before releasing them with no punishment whatsoever. Two other prostitutes made full confessions and were also used as witnesses against the proprietors of the houses, but after their sworn testimony, they were discharged only on the condition that they take the 6:10 p.m. train out of Massena. Like I said, the men who frequented such houses were let off a lot easier than the women providing the services. After that initial raid, Chief Demo said that authorities wanted nothing more than to "clean up this district and make it a place where respectable citizens [could] live at peace," according to the *Republic-Journal*, and he vowed to continue the raids whenever complaints were made.

Elsewhere, Anna Hazard (also spelled Hazzard) was the proprietress of houses of ill fame in the cities of Ogdensburg and Watertown. Her Watertown residence/business was located on River Street, naturally—the city's red-light district. And that address made the news in 1901, after one of Hazard's inmates, as the prostitutes were called, stole money from a man at a saloon in the baron block called the "Bucket of Blood." The *Commercial Advertiser* and the *Watertown Times* of September 18, 1901, gave us our first glimpse of the notorious Anna Hazard and company:

> *The "Bucket of Blood," William Lee's saloon…which is the source of frequent annoyance and labor for the police, was the scene of another unpleasant episode of the half world last night.*
>
> *Yesterday, Adolphus Lalonde of Canton, came to this city and went to Anna Hazard's place at 58 River street. From that resort he took Anna Smith, a fragile fairy of about three hundred* [pounds in] *weight, and they went to Lee's place. There were a number of persons there whose reputations differ in many essentials from that of the late lamented Mrs. Ceasar. The whisky, also, is not above suspicion, and Lalonde had not had very many drinks of it before he hung himself up on a chairback and went to sleep. When he awoke, the dainty Anna was gone. So was $32 that Lalonde claims he had in his pockets. It was learned that the Smith woman had called a hack and left the place in company with Frank Nevils, a brother of the inglorious and thirsty "Pompey."*
>
> *Lalonde went to the police headquarters at 7 last night and told his tale of woe to Sergt. Singleton, who sent Patrolman Gaffney to Anna Hazard's, where he arrested Anna Smith. This morning she was arraigned in city court under the section of the city charter relating to public morality and was sentenced to pay a fine of $25 or serve 30 days in jail. She was committed.*

Then in mid-November 1903, Anna Hazard was arrested on charges of abduction. She waived examination, and the court held her on $800 bond to await grand jury action. Having no means to produce the money for her release, since "business" had apparently not been as good as hoped, she was immediately committed to jail and was indicted by the grand jury in January 1904 for the abduction, and trial was set for March.

According to a lengthy article in the *Watertown Re-Union* of March 12, 1904, Miss Hazard was the keeper of the disorderly house on River Street in Watertown, as well as a house of ill repute in Ogdensburg. On November 6, 1903, Hazard was spotted by Patrolman Frank L. Corey at the train station in Watertown seeing a girl named Jessie off on the northbound train. Corey became suspicious (recognizing Hazard and knowing of her reputation) and brought the woman and the girl before the district attorney, who—after sizing up the situation—secured a warrant for Hazard's arrest. Jessie, as the first witness called for the prosecution, testified that she was sixteen years old and from Gouverneur before she met Anna Hazard. She said that on

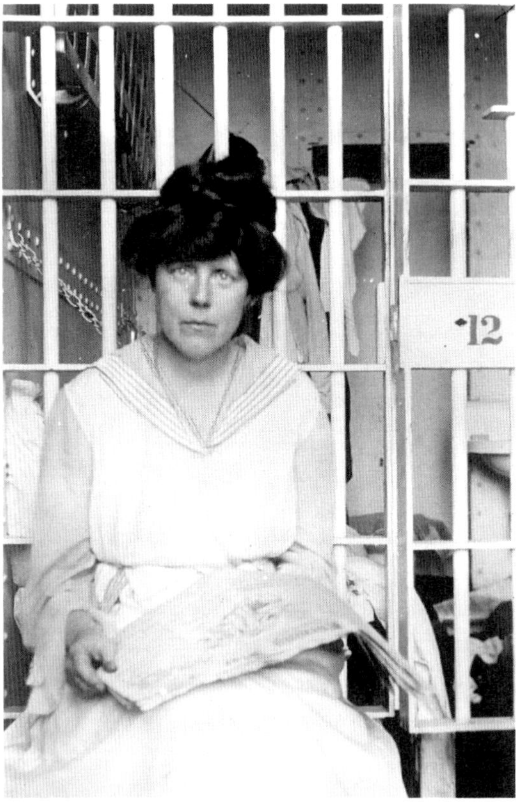

Photograph in the Harris & Ewing Collection, 1917. *Library of Congress Prints and Photographs Division.*

November 6, she was looking for work and was introduced to a bartender named Bowers at the Bucket of Blood saloon on lower Court Street. She accompanied him to a Mrs. Griffin's house on Court Street. (The bartender later played dumb, insisting he had no idea what Anna had planned for Jessie, only that she was looking to hire a girl.) Hazard arrived at Griffin's house shortly thereafter and told Jessie that she could provide her with "good employment and good clothes," according to the *Re-Union*, but Jessie said "no reference was made to a sporting house at that time."

The girl said she had been working as a domestic servant for several prominent families in Watertown, Star Lake and Gouverneur since the age of thirteen, after being released from the Rochester Industrial School. Her parents divorced when she was five, and she had been committed there after being abused by an aunt. She stated that she had never met Miss Hazard before, nor had she known that Hazard operated houses of ill repute. She followed Miss Hazard unquestioningly to the train depot, where Hazard bought her a ticket, telling Jessie that another girl would meet her at the Ogdensburg train station. Hazard was not planning to return to Ogdensburg for a couple more days. It was allegedly there at the train station in Watertown that Hazard finally got around to telling the girl that she was a proprietress of a sporting house (a madam of a brothel) in Ogdensburg and had a cook and another girl in her employ there. At that moment, Officer Corey approached the girl (while Hazard was away buying the ticket) and told her "she would get into trouble with the police, if she went with the Hazzard woman." When Jessie confronted Hazard with that warning, she was told, "I have pull with the Ogdensburg police, and they will make no trouble for you."

Other witnesses included Jessie's father, who corroborated what she had said; Patrolman Corey, who testified as to his conversation with the girl at the train station; Ogdensburg policeman John Sovie, who testified that Hazard was, indeed, the proprietress of a disorderly house in that city (so much for Hazard's statement that she had "pull with the Ogdensburg police"); and Clarence Comstock, the manager of the local Western Union office who produced a message sent by Anna Hazard to her other young prostitute simply saying, "Meet girl at train" on November 6.

After the defense rested, Hazard's attorney moved for her discharge on the grounds of insufficient evidence, but the motion was denied. District Attorney Cobb "strenuously appealed for the upholding of the law in its protection of young women," according to the *Re-Union*, which said:

> *He vividly pictured the enticement of the Cummings girl to the house of prostitution in Ogdensburg, the attractions it had for her, and of her being saved from sinking into the depths of degradation by an officer of the law. His earnest appeal moistened the eyes of many in the court, and tears streamed down the cheeks of a gray-haired juryman.*

Court then recessed for dinner and reconvened at 9:00 p.m., awaiting the verdict. But at 11:00 p.m., the jurymen came back into the courtroom, saying they had not agreed on a verdict and needed some clarification on certain matters. Juryman J.C. Cole, for example, asked, "What is a sporting house?" and said, "If a sporting house is not a house of ill fame, I know what my verdict will be." The judge replied that "it was for the jury to determine what a sporting house is." But the term (sporting house) has long been synonymous with brothel, house of ill repute, bordello, cathouse, whorehouse and gentleman's club. And I'm not sure why the inquiring juror wasn't told as much. Ultimately, Hazard was found "guilty of an attempt at

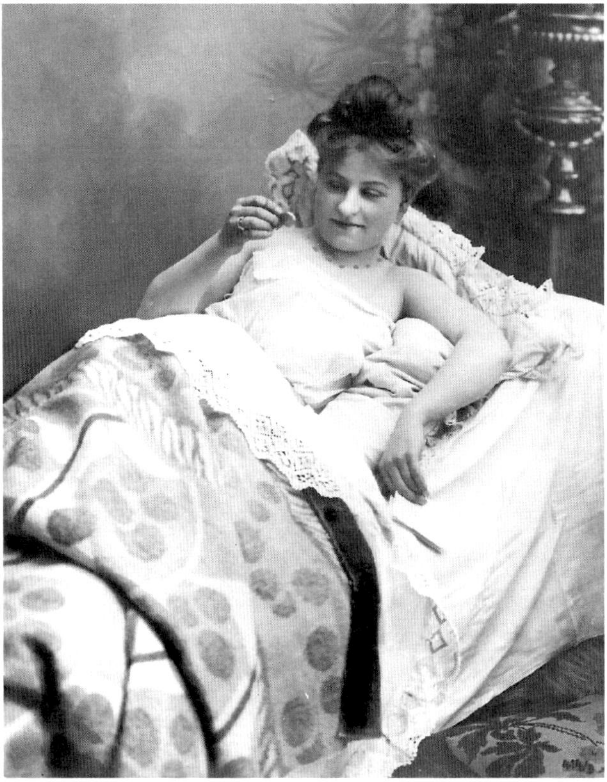

Courtesy of the author.

abduction, with a recommendation of mercy," according to the *Re-Union* of June 22, 1904. Three days later, the paper described her sentencing:

> *At 4 Anna Hazzard, who was convicted by a jury Tuesday morning of an attempt to commit the crime of abduction, was brought before the court for sentence. In answer to questions by the district attorney, she gave the following information: Her name, other than her stage name, is Elizabeth Hodge; was born in Toronto, is 29, and married; has a mother living and was convicted but on one previous occasion and that for keeping a disorderly house.*
>
> *Attorney McCormick, her attorney, asked the leniency of the court in pronouncing sentence and stated that the woman has a brother in St. Louis who desires her to come to that city. He suggested that the court either order her out of town or that a small fine be imposed.*
>
> *The court stated that he thought that some punishment should be inflicted to impress it on the minds of such people and to teach others to let these young girls alone. He sentenced her to six months' imprisonment in the county jail.*

The Man Who Scared His Wife to Death

Sissonville/Potsdam, 1902

apoplexy *n.*
Sudden impairment of neurological function, especially from a cerebral hemorrhage; a stroke. An effusion of blood into a tissue or organ.
—The American Heritage® Stedman's Medical Dictionary

Barney and Rosa Moscow lived in a duplex in Sissonville in 1902 that they rented from George Sisson, who was also Barney's boss at the A. Sherman Lumber Co. (the Sissonville mill where Freddie Brosseau's father worked in a previous story). Moscow was a Frenchman described as being in his mid-fifties, slighter than medium in height, hardworking and hard drinking. He had worked for Sisson at the mill for twenty years and was a familiar fixture in the small community. Rosa was in her mid-forties and heavyset by yesterday's standards; she had reportedly not been in the best of health and was prone to occasional spells that caused her to pass out.

Because the circumstances surrounding the events that transpired on the morning of Sunday, August 3, 1902, were different with each telling of the story, I've decided to tell the version that was first reported, as that often proves to be the most accurate, before the various factions involved spin it to their advantage (defense attorneys, prosecutors, family members, witnesses, media, etc.). According to the *Norwood News* of August 5, 1902, Barney Moscow was in his front yard, drunk and creating a disturbance after returning home from a fishing trip, about 8:00 a.m. His wife was trying to get him to quiet down, so as not to wake the neighbors on the Sabbath.

Moscow took offense in his intoxicated state and attacked her. Fifteen-year-old Melvin Ritchie, who worked with Moscow at the mill, was walking down the road on his way to work and was approaching the Moscow house when he noticed the Moscows quarreling:

> *Suddenly Moscow ran into the house to where his wife was standing in the doorway, striking her in the jaw with his fist and pushing her over. She fell into the house. Mr. Joseph Lamorie, attracted to the screams, ran to the scene, reaching in time to take Moscow away from his wife, who was unconscious. Lamorie and Richie* [sic] *say that Moscow kicked the woman after she fell.*
>
> *Mrs. Moscow was carried to her bed, and medical aid* [was] *summoned. Dr. S. P. Brown of Potsdam arrived and pronounced the woman dying. She did not regain consciousness and died shortly afterward.*

Rosa attempted to fight back. The *Norwood News* reported, "Feeble as she was, [she] made a defense against her assailant" before collapsing on the kitchen floor. That was when Joe Lamorie, her neighbor, arrived, having been summoned by young Ritchie. Lamorie threw Moscow out of the house and called for the physicians, but it was too late. Rosa had died, at first appearances, by apoplexy, a medical term that used to be a catchall for afflictions like ruptured aneurysms, heart attacks and sudden cardiac deaths. At the time of Rosa's passing, "apoplexy" was still being used to describe any sudden death that happened following an episode of unconsciousness, and Rosa had fallen unconscious—with a little help from her abusive husband, who landed a good one on the side of her head. Nevertheless, Coroner Smith of Winthrop performed the autopsy and deemed the death "due to hemorrhage of the brain caused by excitement." I'm no doctor, but couldn't the hemorrhage of the brain have been caused by blunt-force trauma to the head suffered at the hands of her husband as he beat her about the face? Laying the blame for her cerebral hemorrhage on "excitement" rather than on the physical trauma she suffered that morning makes it sound as if Moscow had nothing to do with his wife's sudden death. And that's what Moscow's attorneys were banking on.

It was then that Ritchie ran to Lamorie's house and told him of the situation. The *Advertiser* said that Lamorie found Mrs. Moscow lying on the kitchen floor with her husband standing over her, and when Lamorie asked Barney what he had been doing, "Moscow answered that it was none of his --- ---- business," at which point Lamorie grabbed him by the collar and

Library of Congress Prints and Photographs Division.

physically threw him out. Amazingly, the paper said, "the coroner's inquest Monday disclosed no evidence of foul play." *No evidence of foul play?* But Coroner Smith and Dr. Bridges swore that they found "three marks on the hip near the back, three near the shoulders" and a mark on the lip. They found "a blood clot in the brain proper which weighed about three ounces." Does that count for nothing? Moscow admitted "that there was trouble, but that he had not struck his wife *hard* or with the idea of hurting her, but that she was angry at him for getting up early in the morning and going fishing." He hoped the jury would see *him* as the victim here. And some "expert witnesses" vouched for him, contradicting the findings of the coroner and Dr. Bridges. The *Courier & Freeman* of November 5, 1902, said:

> *Dr. Brown testified that he was summoned to attend the woman and found her apparently suffering from apoplexy, which might occur without*

> *excitement, but was more likely to with…Found no bruises worthy of mention on the woman. Anything tending to increase the action of the heart would render apoplexy liable.*

In other words, if Moscow's left hook didn't kill his wife, then he literally scared her to death by increasing "the action of her heart," causing the apoplexy Brown blamed for her death. The jury blamed the woman's "bad blood vessels" and poor health for causing her death, not the beating, and unanimously found Moscow innocent. The *Courier & Freeman* said, "Moscow promised the jury to stop drinking" before returning home—kind of like a wife beater promising his wife that he'll never beat her again, and we all know how that goes.

Eleven years after Rosa Moscow's untimely death, Barney was still drinking heavily, not surprisingly. On April 24, 1913, he was walking along (or, depending on the source, sitting on) the railroad track near the Ellis Crossing two miles south of Norwood when the 10:13 p.m. northbound train came around a blind bend and struck him. The engineer said he tooted the whistle as soon as he noticed a man on the tracks, but Moscow didn't seem to hear the train. He was thrown twenty feet and died instantly. His identity was determined only by some letters found in his pockets, and the body was delivered to Coroner Smith, who had overseen the autopsy of Moscow's wife. It was a tragic ending to a life cursed by alcohol.

The North Country Gypsy Invasion

1890s–1920s

In the early 1880s, a large wave of Romanian gypsies emigrated from Europe to the United States and Canada, making their presence known throughout Northern New York for the next forty years. Some see gypsies as colorful, free-spirited wanderers who live by opportunity, making the best out of each pit stop, before moving on to the next town. But to many, the word conjures images of trouble-makers and vagabonds drifting from town to unsuspecting town, stealing, begging, telling fortunes and even kidnapping their youth, as in the case of Freddie Brosseau. The North Country of yesteryear experienced both the best and the worst of what these enigmatic nomads had to offer, as the following chronological sample of old local newspaper clippings illustrates.

In October 1902, a party of gypsies was driven out of Jefferson County, according to the *Watertown Re-Union*:

> *About 5:30 o'clock Monday afternoon Sheriff Ballard drove out of the county a band of about 25 Gypsies that had encamped in the town of Pamelia, opposite the city pumping station, and were annoying residents of that vicinity. Three of the women were arrested for fortune telling, but were released. The whole party started overland Monday night for Syracuse.*

While gypsy men were often involved in the trade of horses as a means of making a meager living, the customary trade of gypsy women has historically been fortunetelling, in which they used various means of

Photograph by J. Ellsworth Gross, 1902. *Library of Congress Prints and Photographs Division.*

divining information relevant to one's future, like palm reading, the reading of tea leaves, use of a crystal ball and reading tarot cards and regular cards. But their divination of choice in the late 1800s and early 1900s was palm reading because it required no instruments or objects and could, therefore, be done rather discreetly and inexpensively. The art was taught to gypsy daughters at an early age, as was a gypsy art called *hokkani boro*, or "the great trick," in which an unsuspecting customer was tricked into believing that his money could be doubled if he wrapped a certain amount in a special cloth provided by the gypsy and allowed the gypsy to chant over the bundle before hiding or burying it in an out-of-the-way place, with a promise not to disturb it until the gypsy returned. Typically, the gypsy would return a day or a week later with a similar bundle hidden under her skirt, which contained twice the amount as the original. That way, when she uncovered the original bundle of money, she could discreetly replace it with the new bundle. If the customer fell for that trick, the gypsy would encourage him to wrap a much larger amount of money in the cloth before storing it away as before, and the next time the gypsy came to reveal its contents, she would replace that bundle with a wad of plain old paper cut into the size of dollar bills and wrapped in the same type of cloth. Then, she would leave with the real bundle of cash and never return (having undoubtedly moved on to the next town). Eventually, the customer would figure out that he had been duped.

It was this sort of activity that gave gypsies a bad name, leading to laws in other states that specifically targeted gypsies. Virginia, for example, barred gypsies from fortunetelling in the 1930s; and New Jersey, as recently as the 1980s, created special regulations and licensing requirements specifically intended for gypsy fortunetellers.

In July 1908, the citizens of Antwerp, in Jefferson County, filed a complaint against a large wagon train of gypsies that had "made life a burden to the people around town," according to the *Re-Union*. So the deputy sheriff ordered the seventy-three men, women and children "dressed as they would be at a fair on the midway" to take their ten rigs and leave town, which they promptly did, being used to being turned away. A similar caravan was better received in Cadyville, Clinton County, that same month, according to the *Plattsburgh Daily Republican*, which said, "A band of gypsies visited town on Monday, reading the palms of all that would allow them." The *Watertown Herald* and the *Herald Recorder* a month later described the situation in St. Lawrence County:

> *Potsdam was overrun by gypsies on Wednesday and looked like two or three Durbars at Coney Island rolled into one. Every man in sight was tackled to have his fortune told. The band had a disposition to use the lower end of Main Street as a place for trading horses, but Officer Leahy hustled them on. In Gouverneur, there were reports that several merchants were buncoed out of various sums of money. It is said that one of the gypsy women would accost a man, asking him to permit her to tell his fortune. She would tell him to place a bank note in her hand, while she was working over his palm; and then after completing her work, would reach over and tuck the bill into his pocket. In one or two cases, when the man afterward looked for the bill, it was missing from his pocket. One merchant is said to have lost a $10 bill in this manner.*

In the following years, stories of gypsy trouble came from every county in Northern New York. In the summer of 1909, the good residents of Essex County couldn't decide if they liked them or loathed them. The *Plattsburgh Sentinel* said that when the gypsies passed through Upper Jay one day in mid-June, residents had been warned that "some of them were inclined to take things that did not belong to them," and although nothing was stolen from that village and, in fact, "quite a few [people] rather enjoyed their visit," others "locked their doors, barred their windows and were ready to flee even

Photograph by Fitz W. Guerin. *Library of Congress Prints and Photographs Division.*

to the mountaintops to get out of their way." My guess is that one of the disenchanted residents was the *Sentinel* reporter who submitted the following piece on July 23, 1914:

> *A band of gypsies, about as filthy and generally objectionable lot as could possibly be, got together, struck the town the other day after being driven from town to town on their way south through the county. Their stay in town was short. They were ordered to "move on" by Officer Sheldon, and they gave prompt heed on the order.*

And that's exactly how it was for them, regardless of how many young ones they had to feed or how tired they were from being tossed like hot potatoes from one county to the next. With each stop, they hoped to find temporary job opportunities and a place to set up camp and rest, but their reputations—deserved or not—preceded them, and most towns had little tolerance for them. This *Herald* article from 1916 was a perfect example:

Sheriff Charles C. Hosner was notified Sunday by residents of the section between Chaumont and Reynolds Corners of a band of gypsies which were preparing to camp in that vicinity. Complaint was made by the farmers in that section against the gypsies. The sheriff drove by automobile to the section and ordered them to move on. They were kept moving until they had left the county.

In 1917, the *Plattsburgh Daily Republican* announced, "The familiar sight of a band of gypsies with their countless horses, dogs, and gaily-colored vans is apparently a thing of the past, and no more will we see them slowly trouping through the country, stopping where night overtakes them." Instead, they were travelling in style…in "high-powered and expensive automobiles," when they reached Malone on May 10, 1917. Three such cars full of gypsies arrived in town and set up camp in Chasm Falls. The *Republican* said:

The gypsies were about twenty in number and had the usual quota of small and somewhat soiled children, but no horses and dogs. In Chasm Falls they are said to have done considerable begging and caused a feeling of unrest

Photograph from the National Photo Company Collection. *Library of Congress Prints and Photographs Division.*

> *among the residents of that section of the town...They attempted to beg a chicken from Mrs. Goodman at Chasm Falls and gave as an excuse for the fowl that one of their women had given birth to a child on the night before, and they wished a chicken with which to make the woman some soup. Those who saw the band, however, saw no evidence of a newly born child and were convinced there was none in the camp.*

Local authorities were also notified that a Westville man believed the gypsies passing through Malone had stolen some money from him before they moved on to Chasm Falls. Based on nothing more than the man's suspicion, an officer was dispatched to the Falls, where he arrested five gypsies, who were taken to Malone and examined before the justice of the peace. If there was any truth to the claim, it was never announced in the paper. Two months later, and fifty miles east in West Chazy, a man accused a gypsy maid of stealing from him as well. In that case, the *Plattsburgh Daily Republican* reported that, while telling the man his fortune, "a sly gypsy maid relieved him of a roll of bills amounting to over fifty dollars." Had they learned nothing, in twenty years of similar newspaper accounts, about

Painting by Albert Anker, 1880. *Wikimedia Commons.*

the risks of having their fortunes read by gypsies? The article went on to say that the band of gypsies stopped for just a few hours in Chazy, where the women walked around the village trying to tell fortunes, when "one of them approached [the man] and began to tell his fortune, in the meantime reaching in his pocket and removing about fifty dollars in currency." As soon as he realized his money was missing, the sheriff was notified and sent to locate the gypsies. At the time that article went to print, they had not yet been detained.

I leave you with one final story about gypsies that allegedly took place in 1922 at the Sunrise Hotel, located on the Plank Road in Ellenburg, just west of Plattsburgh. The hotel had, at one point in time, been a "disreputable resort" and was, in fact, featured in another story in this book about prostitution in 1909. In mid-April 1922, a small band of gypsies passed through Clinton County. On April 17, two of the women in the party drove to the hotel, seeking "to tell the fortunes of the women in the house," who happened to be a mother and daughter, Mrs. Riel and Mrs. Rondeau, respectively. The *Plattsburgh Sentinel* said:

> *They got Mrs. Riel upstairs while one of the women engaged the attention of her daughter in the lower part of the house. Part of their plan of their procedure was to find out where the Riel women kept their money. They evidently succeeded, for about 4:30 yesterday afternoon, Sheriff Coffey got a call telling of the loss of over a hundred dollars by Mrs. Biel and $25 by her daughter. This was about an hour after the Gypsies had visited the hotel.*
>
> *The sheriff got busy in an effort to locate the Gypsy band and last evening learned that a party answering the description had driven through Chazy. They were travelling in a covered Reo truck. In the party were two women, a man and several children.*

The next day, the state troopers located the Reo truck and its occupants in Chateaugay and brought them back to Plattsburgh, where they were arraigned before the city judge. When it was determined that the fortunetellers had, in fact, robbed the mother and daughter at the Sunrise Hotel, the leader of the band of gypsies was fined fifteen dollars, and his son was fined ten dollars. The women who took the money were ordered to return it, which they did. The gypsies were then told to leave Clinton County and not to enter Essex County either. They were last seen heading toward Montreal.

The Election Day Massacre in a Town Dubbed "Bloodville"

Saranac Lake, 1902

The case is evidently a vile one from top to bottom, and shows to what degradation and crime demoralization by rum and women leads.
—Malone Farmer, *November 12, 1902*

Orlando Blood was a prominent Saranac Lake landowner and an early mover and shaker who owned the village's popular Blood's Hotel between 1860 and 1883 and for whom Blood Hill (now Lake Street Hill) was named. In June 1888, George Berkley was subleasing the hotel when Charlie Brown, who had been kicked out for his abusive, drunken behavior, returned with a shotgun and killed Berkley on the front porch of his establishment. For years, the village was dubbed "Bloodville," not only because of the illustrious Blood family's contributions to the community, but also because of a tragic incident at Blood's Hotel that made the moniker eerily appropriate. Just as the nickname was beginning to wane, another infamous incident occurred, hampering efforts to shake the ill-omened label.

On election day, November 4, 1902, Allan Mooney, age twenty-five, shot two women to death and injured a man at the house of Fred McClellan on Prospect Avenue—a residence that news articles suggested was a house of ill repute. Mooney had arrived in town two years earlier from Goldsmith, a hamlet in Franklin County, and was employed as a plumber's helper. The *Malone Farmer* described him as "a man of slight build, small in stature, with sandy complexion, hair slightly curly, and peculiar eyes somewhat deformed." When Mooney wasn't working, he was drinking, and he was

Saranac Lake, 1909. Photograph by Detroit Publishing Co. *Library of Congress Prints and Photographs Division.*

known to be "exceedingly disagreeable" (to put it mildly) when drunk. In the days following the murders, local news articles, like one in the *Malone Palladium*, said that he was "jealously in love with Ethel Fayette, or 'Maude,' as she was familiarly known" in Saranac Lake.

Miss Fayette and Viola Middleton were living with Fred McClellan, the latter as his housekeeper, and so was Mooney's nephew, Charles Merrill. Like Mooney, Merrill was also from Goldsmith. Miss Fayette was from Chasm Falls, where she was called Ellen Thomas. So the cast of this sordid script included Fayette, Middleton and McClellan as victims, Merrill as the hero and Mooney as the killer.

Mooney, who was obsessed "with the charms of the Fayette woman, had been staying at the McClellan house for a few days prior to the incident and was considered to be a frequent visitor before that, on account of his interest in Fayette, who had recently moved in. But he wasn't the only man in the house who was smitten with Fayette. So was his very own nephew—and she by him. That didn't sit well with Mooney. On November 4, he had been out riding with the two women of the house and dropped them back off at McClellan's while he returned the rig to the livery stable. When he arrived back at the house, Fayette was with Merrill. According to the *Malone Farmer*, Mooney "wanted McClellan to let him have the woman, but McClellan warned him to stay away, whereupon Mooney told him in substance that he would pay for it and went downtown and bought a .45 caliber revolver and cartridges."

That was one version of what precipitated the murders. In another version, Mooney was so drunk and disruptive that morning that McClellan—whom Mooney had only recently befriended—kicked him out of the house by force, and as in the previous version, Mooney then swore to get revenge on everyone in the house before heading downtown to drink some more, prompting a reporter to later question why a man already drunk out of his mind was still served more liquor.

About five o'clock in the afternoon, Mooney returned to the McClellan house, demanding to be let in. Because he was so drunk, he was refused entrance. So he went around to the back of the house and found that the

Photograph by G.W. Edmondson, 1874. *Library of Congress Prints and Photographs Division.*

rear door was secured shut only with a chair propped up against it, since the lock was broken. Mooney sulked away but returned several hours later to finish his business. Slipping in through the back door, he "was standing in the doorway of a room occupied by McClellan and Viola Middleton, with the revolver in his hands," before anyone knew he had come in. The *Palladium* of November 13, 1902, described the tragic events that unfolded then:

> *Pointing the weapon at McClellan, the fiend cried: "If you have anything to say, say it quick!" McClellan started to rise from the edge of the bed, where he was sitting, when Mooney fired. The first ball struck him in the right breast and glanced off, producing a painful flesh wound. The second and third shots were fired at the Middleton woman, one striking her in the chest and one in the abdomen. She died two or three days later.*
>
> *Not being satisfied with his dastardly act in this part of the house, he repaired to the room of the Fayette woman. The room was in darkness, and Mooney fired one shot in the direction of the bed, the ball passing through the body of the woman, entering just below the heart. She died in about an hour. In the meantime, Merrill, who was in the room of the Fayette woman, had crawled under the bed unnoticed, and when Mooney fired his last shot toward the ceiling, Merrill emerged from his hiding place and grappled*

Photograph by G.W. Edmondson, 1874. *Library of Congress Prints and Photographs Division.*

with Mooney, taking the revolver away from him and holding him until Policeman Moore was summoned.

So Merrill had to restrain his own uncle until police arrived. That had to be a tough spot to be in. The *Malone Farmer* added more details, saying that the room Fayette and Merrill were in had no door and adjoined the room of McClellan and Middleton, separated only "by an arch and portieres which were apart sufficiently for him to see between them" into the bed on which Fayette lay, paralyzed by fear, in the dark. Mooney, in his drunken rage, fired blindly toward the bed, unaware that Merrill had slipped away and was about to subdue him. The coroner's investigation was held at the scene the next day, and Mooney was transferred to the Malone jail, where he was held for murder in the first degree, as his crime was obviously premeditated. Merrill and McClellan were also held, but as material witnesses only. The *Farmer* reported that the Plattsburgh paper said, "McClellan attempted to commit suicide that afternoon about 4 o'clock by drinking carbolic acid, but is still alive and may recover." (He did.)

The community was outraged for a number of reasons, not the least of which was that two women had been gunned down. Besides the fact that a house such as McClellan's was allowed to remain in operation, a man everyone knew was a mean drunk was served alcohol when he had clearly already had too much. And finally, a drunk was able to obtain a revolver with which to perform his terrible deed. The *Malone Farmer* voiced its understandable outrage:

A little well-directed effort some time ago would probably have rid Saranac Lake of the conditions in the McClellan house and saved a big bill of expense to the county.

Shooting affairs and murderous assaults are becoming altogether too frequent hereabouts, and our failure to discover in some cases the assailant and to convict in other cases has created much adverse comment both at home and in neighboring counties. So far as we have been able to learn by hearsay evidence, this case appears to be a clear one. We hope that it will be tried on its merits and on the evidence, regardless of petitions which too often defeat the ends of justice.

The Saranac Lake Forum, according to the *Farmer*, followed suit with its sentiments and released a statement saying:

> *The conditions existing in the house where the* [murders were] *committed were known to the authorities at least 48 hours before the murder. The Fazette* [sic] *woman was arrested the Sunday night before and confined in the jail overnight, only to be released Monday to return to the house. People are now telling on the streets, and were telling just after the murder, that Mooney was a hard drinker and had been right along. Knowing this, as most of the bartenders did, why was he supplied with liquor? The night of the murder, he had not been locked up an hour before he had fallen into a drunken slumber, sleeping until awakened in the morning. When he did wake up, he denied any knowledge of the crime. He is now charged with murder, but the real criminals are the men who sold him the rum, knowing his condition.*

To make matters worse, the forum said, "Officer Moore was on his way to raid the house at the time of the murder, 48 hours after the authorities knew the existing conditions," and implored, "Why the delay?" The trial took place at a special trial term of the Supreme Court beginning May 25, 1903. District Attorney Main represented the people, while Attorney Moore represented Mooney. Moore claimed that his client was susceptible to violent attacks of epilepsy during which he was often unaware of his actions. Furthermore, he had a family history of psychiatric problems, like an aunt who was placed in a Canadian insane asylum and a mother who "was subject to hysterical fits, during which she lost all control of herself," according to the *Farmer* in its trial coverage. Two doctors testified that "Mooney's physical condition was such that, when aroused by a small quantity of liquor, he would become violently insane and unconscious of his acts." Furthermore:

> *From peculiarities of his head, eyes and looks, they would class him as a degenerate who was much more susceptible to insanity than a normal man; that in their opinion, judging from his physical condition, acts, appearance, and talk, he was in such a condition on Nov. 4th that, after having taken a quantity of liquor, he was insane and was not conscious of the acts he was committing.*

On that note, Mr. Moore rested his case, hoping he had demonstrated that his client was an "heir to insanity" and completely unaware of what he had done and, therefore, not guilty. The district attorney then called a number of witnesses, including several relatives, who swore they had never seen Mooney having such attacks, but they agreed he "represented a low type of manhood and possessed certain peculiarities characteristic of degeneracy."

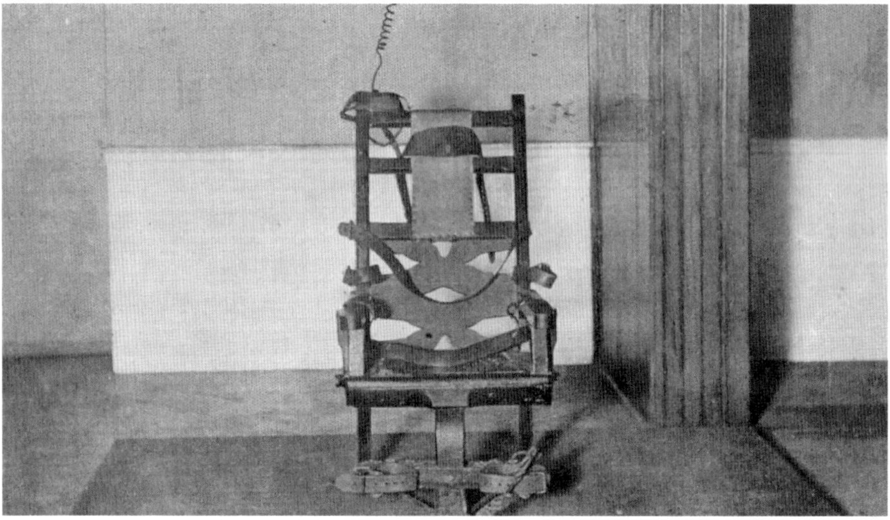

Courtesy of the author.

Their opinion, however, based on his actions and appearance on the night of the murders, was that Mooney was sane "now and at the time of the shooting." The jury agreed and returned the next morning with a verdict of murder in the first degree. Mooney was sentenced to be electrocuted at Dannemora the week of July 6. He didn't flinch when his sentence was handed down but instead thanked the judge courteously before being led away to the "death house" at Dannemora. However, his mother, who was in the courtroom, was "so overcome by the verdict that, on her return home, she had to be carried aboard the train."

On March 3, 1904, the *Malone Palladium* said Mooney was failing in health, ate very little, took no exercise and seemed completely unaware of his surroundings as he sat stoically in his cell. At the time, those who saw him didn't believe he would survive another year in prison. They needn't have worried. Two months later, he went to the electric chair. His body was then placed in a casket and loaded on a train en route for Malone, where he was buried beside his brother and two sisters. The *Malone Farmer* offered this final thought: "The terrible crime for which he [paid the ultimate price] was surrounded by all the accessories of moral debauchery and is one of the sequences which so often occurs in connection with that sort of life."

The Girl Who Was Traded for Chickens

Schuyler Falls, 1908

Late one chilly afternoon in November 1908, a young girl—barefoot, filthy and scantily clad—showed up at the Lavalley residence in Cadyville seeking shelter. She said her name was Annie and that her parents, Abraham and Mary Terrier of Schuyler Falls, had "put her out." How do you kick a ten-year-old child out? From the condition of the girl, the eviction from her so-called home by her so-called parents was apparently a blessing in disguise. One glance at their diminutive visitor and the Lavalleys knew that Humane Officer Hennessy was needed. While modern humane officers specialize in animal cruelty, in the early 1900s, it was, as one paper called it, the "noble work of preventing cruelty to [both] children and animals." It was the humane officer's job to enforce anti-cruelty laws within his jurisdiction. In those days, there were no government agencies to oversee the welfare of children, so Hennessy acted as a forerunner of today's caseworker for the New York State Department of Social Services–Child Protective Services division. He had undoubtedly seen his share of shocking situations, due to the nature of his work, but this was one case he would never forget.

Hennessy questioned the child and the neighbors of her caretakers but was unable to speak with her real parents because her biological father had left several years earlier, after an argument with her real mother. Then, shortly thereafter, Annie's mother died, and Annie became an orphan—and a vulnerable target for predators, like (in her case) gypsies, pimps and child abusers, in that order. Thus, the girl's actual name, the humane officer soon learned, was Annie Ashline of Keeseville, not Annie Terrier of Schuyler

Postcard published by T.P. & Co., New York. *Courtesy of the author.*

Falls. She had somehow fallen in with a band of gypsies passing through the area at the time of her mother's death, and although they provided the most basic necessities of life for the short time that she was with them, they did her no favors. In fact, they did the unthinkable, selling her to a "man of alleged ill repute near Redford" for fifty cents—*fifty cents*—the equivalent of twelve dollars today. When he was finished with her, he took her to the Terrier home and traded her for a half dozen chickens, placing her value at next to nothing—and things were about to get worse for her.

While in the care of the Terriers, neighbors told Hennessy that the child was regularly beaten, which they called "flogging" back then, provided with but little clothing and sent through the snow barefoot to the woods to fetch firewood for the family. The *Ticonderoga Sentinel* of December 3, 1908, said she had been "buffeted from pillar to post and [had] been frightfully abused," until the day the Terriers kicked her out and the Lavalleys contacted Humane Officer Hennessy on the girl's behalf. Annie was committed to the St. Vincent's orphan asylum in Troy. The *Sentinel* said that at least the investigation "resulted in putting the unfortunate waif in a place where she will receive the care and education which has thus far in her life been lacking."

Warrants were issued for the arrest of both Mr. and Mrs. Terrier, "on a charge of endangering the morals of the child, under section 289," according to the *Press Republican*. Mary Terrier was held "under $100 bail, to appear before Justice Emery," and Abraham Terrier, while he could not initially be found, did manage to show up in time for his and his wife's arraignment a few days later. Incredibly, Justice R.H. Emery released the contemptible couple, saying the charge brought against them by Humane Officer Hennessy was lacking in evidence to support it. They were free to go.

Perhaps if the good justice had walked a mile in the child's shoes, he might have come to a different conclusion. But he hadn't been subjected to the deeds of a man of ill repute against a frail little body; he hadn't felt the familiar sting of a whip or been chained to a porch like a dog; and he hadn't experienced the shame of being sold for a mere fifty cents before being traded for six lousy chickens. If none of that is endangering a child's morals, then what is?

By the Promise of Pretty Clothes

Northern New York, 1901–1909

Here's something we don't see in the North Country anymore: white slavery, also known as forced prostitution. As previously mentioned, in the early twentieth century, there seemed to be houses of ill repute in every neighborhood, in every town, in every county of Northern New York. And where there were houses of prostitution, there was a need for someone(s) to provide the services that kept the houses in business. Those "someones" were typically young French-Canadian women lured across the border by the promise of good money, pretty clothes and independence in the United States. By the time a girl got off the train in Watertown, Ogdensburg, Massena or Plattsburgh, it was often too late to warn her of what she was really about to get herself into. If she was lucky, an observant law enforcement officer might intervene just in the nick of time.

On February 23, 1909, two young French Canadian women named Clara and Julia, twenty-one and twenty-six, respectively, arrived in Ogdensburg on a train from Ottawa to Watertown. Immigration inspector Joseph A. Conaty suspected something when he saw them, as he was well aware of investigations into "white slave" traffic that were being quietly conducted at the time. When he questioned the girls, one of them offered that they were on their way to visit their "Aunt Lesperance" on River Street in Watertown, not realizing that the immigration officer was very familiar with the reputation of River Street. It was certainly not the most wholesome place for two young girls to visit. But Conaty allowed the girls to continue on their journey and immediately notified the authorities in Watertown to

Courtesy of the author.

be on the lookout for two girls heading that way who might find themselves in "that" kind of trouble.

Six days later, the girls, sure enough, were found at Ida Lewis's place at 42 River Street. Lewis was a well-known proprietress of a house of ill repute in the city. When Inspector Conaty and deputy United States marshal E.C.J. Smith arrived in Watertown that evening, they met Captain Wood and Lieutenant Edghill of the Watertown Police Department, and about nine o'clock, Ida Lewis was arrested on "charges of violating the immigration laws in bringing two girls into this country and harboring them for immoral purposes." The girls were taken to the police station, where they were held as witnesses on $500 bail each. United States commissioner John Rogers was called to the courthouse, arriving an hour later, and read the charges to Miss Lewis before setting bail at $2,000. Since she couldn't come up with that much money that quickly, she spent the night in jail, to await the next morning's preliminary examination. The *Daily Journal* of March 12, 1909, said:

> *Tonight's arrest is the most important of its kind made here in many months. The results will probably be far-reaching before the investigation comes to an end. Two letters written in French have been found and are now in the hands of the police. The information gathered from their contents, it is alleged, is that a man has been scouring Canada in securing young French Canadian girls for the houses of prostitution of this and other cities.*

The next day, there was another arrest in the case. Laura Roland (aka Lesperance and Rollin) was Lewis's housekeeper and the alleged "Aunt Lesperance" of whom the two girls spoke. She had arrived from Ottawa about six weeks earlier. She, too, was charged with violating the immigration laws, and bail was set at $2,000. Both women secured George Lawyer as their attorney, and both were ordered held by the United States commissioner at Auburn to await the action of the federal grand jury in April. Lewis got out on bail, but Roland was held. According to the *St. Lawrence Republican*, on April 6, both women "decided to throw themselves on the mercy of the court after pleading guilty." Miss Lewis was sentenced to pay $250 and serve two years at the Auburn Women's Prison; however, the prison sentence would be waived, she was told, *if* she promised "that she would never again conduct a house of ill fame." But if she did get caught operating a house of ill fame again, a suspended sentence of one year in prison would immediately take effect.

One source says that Miss Roland was fined $100 and was also sentenced to serve two years at the women's prison. For whatever reason, she was not offered the same sweet deal as Miss Lewis. She had to serve a prison sentence, according to that source. Yet another source, the *Plattsburgh Sentinel*, said she "was more fortunate than [Lewis] and escaped with a fine of $250, which she paid." Whichever the case, both women fared better than a man named Rice, who was charged under similar circumstances in a separate Clinton County case at the same time.

Frank Rice was the keeper of the disreputable resort called the Sunrise Hotel, mentioned earlier in this book. It was located on the old Plank Road in Ellenburg, just west of Plattsburgh. On March 8, 1909, immigration officer James Yale of Rouses Point charged Frank Rice with violating Section 3 of the Immigration Act for "importing from Canada two young alien women—Blanche and Jennie—for immoral purposes." Sound familiar? In this case, the two young women were also arrested and charged with "illegally coming across the line," according to the *Plattsburgh Sentinel* of March 12, 1909. The paper said:

> *Rice had left here on the noon train and gone to Montreal, where he secured the white slaves and returned on the night train with them. Officer Yale was on duty on the train and, after closely questioning the girls, became convinced that they were unlawfully entering the United States. He followed them to* [Plattsburgh] *and kept close watch on them while they were in a restaurant eating lunch. Rice next secured a rig and started with the girls for the resort. The officers followed in another rig, and as Rice's rig stopped on the way, the officers reached the Sunrise first. They had been there only a few minutes when Rice drove up. It was an easy matter to secure the evidence necessary to make a strong case against Rice, and Mr. Yale then appeared upon the scene and the arrests followed.*

Rice and the two girls were locked up about two o'clock in the morning, and the next day they were taken before United States Commissioner Gilliland. Each entered a plea of not guilty. Rice's examination was set for

Courtesy of the author.

two days later. Assistant United States attorney H.E. Owen of Port Henry conducted the examination for the prosecution and called in two witnesses: immigration inspector James Hale of Rouses Point and Blanche, one of the girls the accused had brought over from Canada. No witnesses were called for the defense, and bail was fixed at $2,500, since the maximum penalty for the crime could not exceed a $5,000 fine or five years in prison (or both). Because he could not come up with such an exorbitant amount, Rice remained in jail until April 6, when he was taken to Syracuse to face the grand jury. Nearly two weeks after the arrests, commissioner Gilliland discharged the girls, Blanche and Jennie, who had also been unable to secure the necessary bail for their release, but they remained in jail by order of United States District Court Judge Ray, as witnesses against their would-be employer. The *Plattsburgh Sentinel* of March 26, 1909, said the two made sworn statements "as to the inducements [Rice] made them to come to Plattsburgh."

After providing their testimony before Judge Ray, the two Canadian women were ordered deported back to Montreal, and according to the *Sentinel*, the "Canadian officers have signified their intention to take up the matter, and the pair [would be] arrested as soon as they [reached] the Dominion." As for Rice, he decided to plead guilty and ask for the mercy of the court. He was ordered to pay a fine of $1,000 and to serve three years in the United States penitentiary in Atlanta, Georgia.

That year, immigration inspector David Lehrhaupt said enough is enough and became a one-man sensation, when he set about "making investigations in all cities throughout the state, finding and deporting all alien girls who [were] in houses of ill-fame," according to the *Times Re-Union*. And he had his eye particularly on Watertown's notorious River Street. That year he deported, among others, a Canadian woman named Alda Rol, who went by the "stage name" of "Margaret Chard." Rol was arrested at 56 River Street in a house of ill repute operated by Clara Edgar. Detective Singleton acted on information provided by Lehrhaupt when he made the arrest in August 1909. Rol told Singleton she was twenty-six years old and from Pennelton, Ontario, and that she had worked at various brothels on River Street since her arrival two years before. Like many before her, she had the option of jail time or deportation and chose the latter.

It's hard to imagine a more wicked line of work, yet somehow young women by the hundreds were drawn into the dark world of white slavery right here in Northern New York, lured by dishonest proprietors who glamorized prostitution with the promise of pretty clothes, stage names—as if they were on Broadway—and lucrative job opportunities.

Girl with the Evil Eye

Hogansburg, 1912

Tense excitement prevails at the little Indian village of St. Regis, where people are living in horrible dread inspired by the accusations leveled against Loleta "Lola" Razon, a native girl of 15 who is believed to possess an evil eye, and to whose powers of witchery are attributed the madness of dogs and death of livestock.
—Courier & Freeman, *July 12, 1912*

There was something about Lola Razon, an Indian girl who allegedly lived on (and was kicked off) the St. Regis Mohawk Indian Reservation in 1912. It seemed that whatever she laid her eyes upon, be it a tub of milk or a dog, it immediately went bad…or mad. And when her tribe was unable to exorcize the imagined demons from the child, she was quickly graded a "black witch." According to the *Courier & Freeman* of August 3, 1921:

> *In the olden times, there were three classes of witches. The black witch was a harmful affair, and the white witch was a helpful spirit. Then there was the*

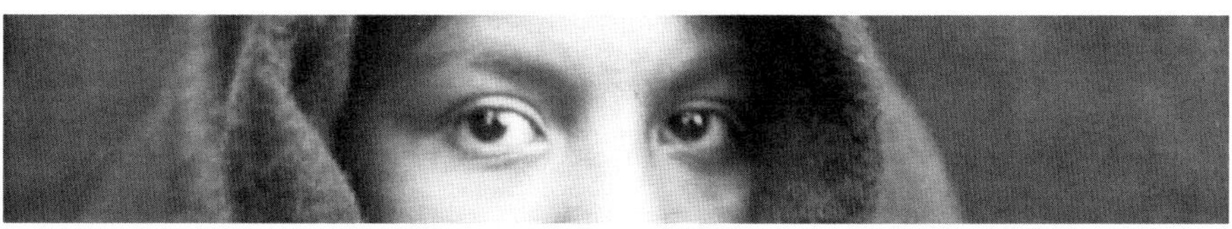

Photograph taken by Edward S. Curtis, 1916. *Wikimedia Commons.*

> *gray witch who was sometimes harmful and sometimes helpful. Indictments against persons accused of witchcraft had to state the complexion of the spirit that bewitched.*

By "complexion," they meant: was she a black witch, a white witch or a gray witch? Color made all the difference. A black witch was a menace to society, and the possibility of a real, live black witch (with an evil eye, no less) in our midst became big news in 1912—so big, in fact, that all the local papers (the *Courier & Freeman*, the *Ogdensburg Advance* and *St. Lawrence Weekly Republican*, the *Plattsburgh Sentinel*, the *Chateaugay Recorder* and *Franklin County Democrat* and the *Commercial Advertiser*, to name a few) carried the story from April through July of that year. But the story of Lola did not originate in the North Country. Rather, it all began a year earlier and three thousand miles away, according to a story that started with the following teaser: "A mite of an Indian girl, fifteen years old, has recently completed one of the most remarkable escapes recorded in the annals of Indian life in the southwest."

That girl, Loleta Razon, a Plute Indian of the Coachella Valley, had been caught gazing at a pan of milk. Her tribesmen noted, to their horror, that the milk then turned sour. Lo and behold, several members of the tribe soon became stricken with a mild illness, and dogs near the shack she lived in with her father occasionally "made the night hideous with their howls." Rather than blame it simply on milk that had gone bad by natural means, the tribe blamed the child and called in its medicine men. According to the *Commercial Advertiser* of January 10, 1911, they attempted to perform an exorcism "with weird rites" to rid the girl of the evil spirits, but their efforts were futile, and "the medicine men then solemnly proclaimed Loleta a witch."

> *Warnings were constantly given not to let her shadow fall upon any member of the tribe or upon their property. A grave council was held by the braves. They decided she must be strangled to death. Loleta heard of her intended fate. She crawled away into the desert. Then, for hours she raced toward the sacred springs in the valley of Guamachi ("a place of plenty to eat"), now known as San Bernardino valley, which offered a cure for witchcraft. She believed the verdict of the medicine men against her was just, but if she could just reach the sacred springs, she would be cleansed.*

So the young girl who was shunned by everyone she knew chose to run for her life, as perilous a journey as it was. She traveled 150 miles over "the most desolate and forbidding sections of the desert and mountain country known" on foot. And by the time she reached her intended destination, she had not eaten and had barely drunk a thing for three days, making her "a mere skeleton of her former self." The *Advertiser* described how the child was taken in by kindhearted squaws, and all seemed well—until they learned of her identity from her own tribe, which was hot on her heels. Just when they were about to capture her, an Indian agent named Royce came to her rescue. He had heard of her death sentence from trusted Indian sources. The article closed by saying that Royce "took her to an Indian school, where she is now."

That was January 1911. Either agent Royce brought Lola all the way across the continent to Northern New York where the same exact thing again happened to the child, or the local news media fell victim to yesteryear's version of an internet hoax, because a year after Lola's rescue, she showed up on the St. Regis Mohawk Indian Reservation at Akwesasne—or at least all the newspapers around here said she did. The story of her forbidden powers and amazing escape from the California tribe is almost identical to the story of her escape from the St. Regis Indian reservation, as you can see from the following article in the *Chateaugay Record* of April 5, 1912, which offered a disclaimer, of sorts, by saying right up front, "The following tale is going the rounds of the newspapers, and we reproduce it for what it is worth." The only changes, really, are those that would give it a local flair.

> *High up in the Luzerne mountains is a mite of an Indian girl, 15 years of age, who has recently completed a remarkable escape from the St. Regis Indian reservation, which is situated in Franklin County, about three miles from the Canadian border. For many long miles she fled through the mountain country to reach the home of John Barlette, a halfbreed, about five miles from the village of Luzerne. She had been for more than three days without food, her feet were frozen, and her clothes in rags. Lola Razon was her name on the reservation before she was suspected of being an evil spirit. After that they called her "Black Witch" and she was transformed in a day into an object of dread.*
>
> *The girl was born on the St. Regis farms. Her life was not different from that of the rest of the children until a few weeks ago, when her uncle discovered that one of his horses she had looked at dropped dead. Later, several of the children she had played with were taken sick, and the dogs on occasions had acted queer, and would gather near her father's house and make the night hideous with their howls. Medicine men were consulted. With their arts, they tried in vain to disperse the "evil spirits," and they*

> *solemnly proclaimed Lola a witch. The squaws instructed their children to shun the girl. Warnings were constantly given not to let her shadow fall upon any member of the tribe or upon the horses or hogs. A grave council was held by the chiefs. They decided she must leave, and she started to find her uncle, John Bartlette. Last fall the Bartlettes moved from Glens Falls to Luzerne mountain, where they are now getting splints for basket making. The little girl says she had a good start toward an education, and that she wished to become a teacher, and she hopes the superstition of her people would die out in time. Mr. Bartlett says the girl would be well taken care of in his home. Lola is a remarkably pretty child, and very intelligent for her years. She has no idea why they think she is a witch, unless it was by a few simple tricks she performed for the children and the grown folks.*

Well, at least the local tribe didn't put a death sentence on the poor child's head! Regardless of whether Lola ever really existed or ever ventured from the Southwest (where the story originated) to the Northeast, the story was wicked in its sensationalism. Catchy old titles from local newspapers included, "Think Girl Has an Evil Eye: Indians are Troubled About Maiden," "Believe in Witches" and "Say She Is 'Black Witch'—Young Indian Girl Accused of Causing Sickness and Death on the Reservation." Most people reading those articles were unaware of the very same story having been told in California a full year earlier. There was nothing in the local articles to suggest that it was untrue, so you really can't blame the people (or the newspapers) for falling victim to such a hoax—if this was, in fact, a hoax.

Whether Lola ever existed, the fear of black witchcraft was alive and well in the North Country at the time, so the gullible public was all too ready to believe the story of the girl with the evil eye. And they were all too quick to rid their neighborhoods of others suspected of witchcraft. According to the *St. Lawrence Republican* in 1904, a Lisbon woman suspected of witchcraft "was seized by a frenzied rabble and thrown upon a pile of her furniture, which was then set on fire. Fortunately," the article said, "the police intervened in time to save the woman's life."

So the Devil Would Leave Him Alone

Westport/North Hudson, 1975

Then Jesus was led by the Spirit up into the desert to be tempted by the devil. After forty days and nights he was very hungry…Then the devil let him alone, and angels came to him and took care of him.
—*Verses 1 and 11, Chapter 4, Book of Matthew,* New Testament

At 1:30 a.m. on May 24, 1975, state police at Westport received a call that a vagrant, possibly armed, was lumbering along the side of Route 9N. When they responded to the call, they found a lanky young, long-haired man struggling to walk with chains wrapped around him from head to toe. His ragged clothes were soiled, and he smelled of urine and sweat. Heavy-duty chains under his clothing ran helter-skelter around his ankles, neck and shoulders. And one bloodied hand was adorned with a broken handcuff, offering a clue to the man's desperate struggle to free himself. Investigators would soon discover why his voice was so hoarse that he could barely speak when he tried to respond to their questions.

The state police learned that the peculiar man was a native of New York City with an extensive criminal record. Five years earlier, he had been charged with incest in the city. A year before that, he was charged with possession of a weapon, and just before he fled to Northern New York, he had been charged with assault. In Elizabethtown and in the town of Peru, he had been arrested for hitchhiking, and he had been charged with assault in Malone, as well. In his mind, he felt he had sinned so badly that even years of on-and-off incarceration had not been enough punishment to cleanse his soul.

Library of Congress Prints and Photographs Division.

The man told investigators that he had bound himself in chains deep in the woods of Westport, where nobody could see or hear him, as a sort of self-penance. He planned to fast for forty days and nights (like Jesus in the Book of Matthew) and to chain himself to the trees and toss away the keys to that end. But with the ravenous mosquitoes and unrelenting hunger pangs, he lasted just three days—three excruciating days of screaming for help where nobody could possibly hear him. Finally, he grabbed a stone and smashed through the handcuffs on his wrist to break it. Then he stumbled out onto the highway and was spotted by a passerby, who phoned the police.

A mental health evaluation revealed that the man was suffering from feelings of "indifference, withdrawal, delusions of persecution, omnipotence, and hallucinations," according to seasoned author and reporter Barney Fowler in his *Adirondack Album, Volume Two*. Nevertheless, he was released. There was no crime with which the authorities could charge or hold him, and he was not considered violent or dangerous at the time to anyone but himself. Thus, the man who was hellbent on creating his self-imposed purgatory in which to atone for his sins was released. Again. Even with an extensive criminal background and less-than-ideal mental health evaluation. Over and over again, the man was allowed to slip through the cracks of the criminal justice and mental health systems, even after telling the town justice that the "next time" he would do it right—"it" being the forty-day fast. He promised he would go out in the woods again, but this time, he would chain himself up, well away from any loose rocks he might grab in a moment of weakness to free himself. If his vow to authorities was a desperate cry for help, it wasn't heard any more than his screams of agony in the woods had been.

Five months later, a hunter walked about a mile into the woods off the Northway in North Hudson when he stumbled upon what he first thought was a deer skull. Closer inspection proved it was a human skull, and the police were summoned. When they arrived on the scene, the words of Westport's "man in chains" came back to haunt them. Scattered among the remains were shoes, cigarettes, matches, a writing tablet, pens, a duffel bag, canteens, plastic bags and, of course, more chains. The man's ankles were both padlocked to one tree, while his handcuffed wrists were chained around another tree, giving him very limited movement—only enough slack to stand, sit and lie down. A metal detector found six keys that had been tossed eleven feet away from the body by the deceased, likely to ensure there would be no turning back this time. Even though no identification was found with

Photo by Barney Fowler. Courtesy of Adirondack Album, Volume Two.

the remains—and the body was in an advanced state of decomposition—the size thirteen shoes still bound to the tree in chains were the size the man from New York City wore, and the chains were similar to those they had found with him several months earlier.

The victim was wearing a pair of work pants over long johns, two thermal undershirts topped by a regular shirt, a suit coat and a three-quarter-length coat. But all the warmth and protection from the elements (and mosquitoes) that his choice of clothing afforded him were pointless if he was going to starve himself to death anyway. The autopsy showed no signs of violence, like broken bones or stab wounds, which added more weight to the theory that the man in chains had locked himself up intentionally and thrown away the keys. Local investigators contacted the New York City Police Department and were told that the man in question had not been seen for several months. They obtained his dental chart and X-rays and forwarded them to a doctor in Elizabethtown, who made a positive identification of the man. It *was* the same man who had vowed to police that he would do it right the next time. And he did.

The authorities insisted they had had no reason to hold the man any longer than they did following a mental exam that they admitted was "not elaborate" because the exam showed the disturbed man did not pose a threat to anyone. One officer said that because the deceased had tied himself to a tree five months earlier and had managed to struggle and break free when he decided he was thirsty, it showed that he had "some sort of desire to live," according to the *Lake Placid News* of October 30, 1975. You can sugarcoat it any way you like, but the bottom line is, a man who desperately needed help—who literally screamed for help—was dismissed by those who could have offered it. It was a tragic demise for a tortured soul who only ever wanted the devil to leave him alone so the angels would come and take care of him. I trust they are now.

Bibliography

Books and Reports

Everts, L.H. *History of St. Lawrence Co., New York with Illustrations and Biographical Sketches of Some of Its Prominent Men and Pioneers.* Philadelphia, PA: L.H. Everts & Co., 1878.

Farnsworth, Cheri. *Adirondack Enigma: The Mysterious Life and Deprived Intellect of North Country Wife Killer Henry Debosnys*. Charleston, SC: The History Press, 2010.

———. *Alphabet Killer: The True Story of the Double Initial Murders.* Mechanicsburg, PA: Stackpole Books, 2010.

———. *Haunted Northern New York*. Vol. 4. Utica, NY: North Country Books, 2010.

———. *Murder & Mayhem in Jefferson County*. Charleston, SC: The History Press, 2011.

———. *Murder & Mayhem in St. Lawrence County*. Charleston, SC: The History Press, 2010.

Madden, R.R. *The Literary Life and Correspondence of the Countess of Blessington.* New York: Harper & Brothers, 1855.

Revai, Cheri. *The Big Book of New York Ghost Stories*. Mechanicsburg, PA: Stackpole Books, 2009.

———. *Haunted Northern New York*. Utica, NY: North Country Books, 2002.

Newspapers

Adirondack Daily Enterprise. "Police Hero Prevented Blood Legacy." April 4, 1985.

Adirondack News. "Murder at Saranac Lake." November 8, 1902.

———. "Noted Horse Thief." October 28, 1893.

———. Note regarding Allan Mooney. November 15, 1902.

———. Note regarding Lon Clark. June 30, 1906.

Adirondack Record-Elizabethtown Post. "Death Blocks Any Solution of Man's Life." March 24, 1932.

Cape Vincent Eagle. "John A. Payne, One of the Lincoln Conspirators." February 26, 1914.

———. "Southern Traitor Victim of Maple Island Murder." April 19, 1923.

———. "Story of Hermit of Maple Island Still Thrills Folks of St. Lawrence River Area." December 22, 1927.

Chateaugay Record. "Armed Negro Shot Down in Woods Fight." March 11, 1932.

———. "Claimed She Was a Witch." April 5, 1912.

———. "Saranac Lake Tragedy." November 14, 1902.

———. "Wild Man Captured." February 16, 1912.

Commercial Advertiser. "A Canton Man Robbed." September 18, 1901.

———. "Condemned as a Witch." January 10, 1911.

———. Note regarding alleged wild man. August 30, 1921.

———. "A Potsdam Tragedy." August 6, 1902.

———. "Treasure Isle on St. Lawrence." April 11, 1916.

———. "Treasure Isle on St. Lawrence." September 16, 1924.

Courier & Freeman. "Body Snatchers Buried in Field." October 5, 1938.

———. "Cemetery Markers Near W. Stockholm Recall Activity of Grave Snatchers." October 13, 1948.

———. County Court: Eamon Gets Eight Years and Moscow is Acquitted. November 5, 1902.

———. "Frederick Brosseau Found." August 20, 1913.

———. "Grades of Witches." August 3, 1921.

———. "Mrs. Celia Brosseau." August 30, 1916.

———. "Noted Grave Robbers Buried Near Winthrop." April 20, 1938.

———. Note regarding Moscow death. April 24, 1913.

———. Note regarding Tarring and Feathering of Mrs. Bert Covey. August 14, 1895.

———. "Ring Recalls Old Crime." June 14, 1916.

———. "Think Girl Has an Evil Eye." July 3, 1912.
———. "Treasure Island Legend." October 7, 1914.
———. "White Slave Trade." March 10, 1909.
Daily Journal. "A Hermit Murderer." April 18, 1898.
———. "A Woman Tarred and Feathered." July 31, 1895.
———. "Another Wild Man." August 30, 1869.
———. "Grand Jury Hears Evidence: Important Case Which Originated at Ogdensburg." April 8, 1909.
———. "Manslaughter in Second Degree: The Charge Against Barney Moscow of Sissonville." August 5, 1902.
———. "Moscow Held for Trial." August 7, 1902.
———. Note regarding wild man in Hermon. December 11, 1874.
———. Note regarding wild man near Ogdensburg. November 20, 1880.
———. "Where is Freddie?" October 30, 1896.
———. "Woman is Arrested: Ogdensburg Officers Have Alleged White Slave Case." March 12, 1909.
Essex County Republican. "Horse Thief Arrested." December 30, 1910.
———. "Lunatic or Criminal Found Near Keeseville." November 19, 1920.
———. "Shoot 'Wild Man' at Bay in Adirondacks." March 11, 1932.
———. "Wild Man Says He Left Clinton Prison in June." November 22, 1912.
Fort Covington Sun. "Another Shooting Affair." November 29, 1902.
Franklin Gazette. Note regarding Lon Clark. November 3, 1893.
———. Note regarding Lon Clark. March 23, 1894.
———. Note regarding Lon Clark. March 1, 1895.
Gouverneur Free Press. "Looking for Long Lost Son." August 20, 1913.
Lake Placid News. "Horse Thief Takes Life by Drinking Poison." July 6, 1923.
———. "Hunters Discover Chained Skeleton." October 30, 1975.
Malone Farmer. "Held for Murder." November 12, 1902.
———. "Home Matters." December 3, 1902.
———. "Mooney Guilty of Murder in First Degree." May 27, 1903.
———. Note regarding wild man in Benson. October 19, 1904.
———. "Suppressed Details About the Saranac Lake Murder." November 26, 1902.
Malone Palladium. "Lon. Clark, Ex-Horse Thief." December 22, 1898.
———. Note regarding Allan Mooney. March 3, 1904.
———. Note regarding Allan Mooney. March 24, 1904.
———. Note regarding Lon Clark. March 22, 1894.
———. Note regarding Lon Clark. October 4, 1906.

———. "The Saranac Lake Murder." November 13, 1902.
———. "Should Have Stopped at One Hundred." October 25, 1894.
Massena Observer. "Amherst's Chest of Gold May Still Be in River." March 15, 1934.
———. "Golden Cache at Treasure Island." September 24, 1914.
———. "Recalling an Old Potsdam Tragedy." August 21, 1913.
———. "Treasure Isle on St. Lawrence." February 2, 1928.
———. "Wedding Ring Recalls Crime." June 8, 1916.
———. "What Became of Daniel Murdock." March 22, 1917.
Moffat, George. "Gold at Long Sault." *Massena Observer*, July 18, 1974.
New York Times. "Girl Tarred and Feathered." September 14, 1912.
———. "Woman Tarred and Feathered." July 31, 1895.
Norwood News. "Brosseau Missing." September 10, 1913.
———. "Murder at Sissonville." August 5, 1902.
———. Note regarding Bertha Covey. October 29, 1895.
———. Note regarding Mrs. Bert Covey. August 20, 1895.
———. "Outrage at Jayville." August 13, 1895.
———. "Potsdam Young Man Found After 17 Years." August 20, 1913.
Ogdensburg Advance. "Believe in Witches." June 27, 1912.
———. "Kidnapped 17 Years Ago." August 21, 1913.
———. Note regarding disappearance of Freddie Brosseau. November 19, 1896.
———. Note regarding Mrs. Bert Covey. August 8, 1895.
———. Note regarding sporting house. November 3, 1898.
———. "Strange Legend of Stockholm Man of Half a Century Ago." March 15, 1917.
———. "Why Named Treasure Island." September 17, 1914.
Ogdensburg Journal. "Mysterious Kidnapping Case May Be Solved Through Efforts of Priest." August 21, 1913.
———. "Treasure Island to Be Flooded by River Projects." August 23, 1954.
———. "Two Grave Robbers Lie Buried Near Winthrop." April 18, 1938.
Ogdensburg Republican-Journal. "Aged Man Found Hanging to Tree in Franklin County." July 11, 1919.
———. "History of Treasure Island Recalled by Darrow's Death." September 19, 1924.
———. "Judge Orders Women to Go From Massena." May 1, 1923.
———. "Wild Man Terrorizes Villagers Near Malone." September 10, 1921.
Plattsburgh Daily Press. "City and Vicinity News." February 19, 1919.

———. Note regarding Frank Rice. April 6, 1909.
———. "Posse Kills 'Wild Man' of Adirondacks." March 7, 1932.
Plattsburgh Daily Republican. "Enter the 1917 Automobile Gypsy in Franklin County." May 10, 1917.
———."7 Gypsies Arrested Here Soon Released." October 8, 1925.
———. "Told Fortune; Took His Roll: Gypsy Maid Relieves West Chazy Resident of Fifty Dollars." July 20, 1917.
Plattsburgh Press. Note regarding Rainbow Lake wild man. November 19, 1909.
———. "Sold Into Slavery – Ten-Year-Old Girl Rescued from Abuse." December 1, 1908.
Plattsburgh Press-Republican. "Local Man Gets Suspended Term in City Court." September 23, 1955.
Plattsburgh Republican. Note regarding Abraham Terrier. December 5, 1908.
———. Note regarding gypsies in Cadyville. August 1, 1908.
———. Note regarding Mrs. Bert Covey. August 3, 1895.
———. Notice regarding tramps. November 12, 1881.
———. "The Rouses Point Canteen." August 10, 1907.
Plattsburgh Sentinel. "The Burglary at Peru." December 13, 1878.
———."Claim Gypsies Robbed Them of Sum of Money." April 18, 1922.
———. "Girls Held on Court Order." March 26, 1909.
———. "Gypsies Ordered to Leave Clinton County." April 18, 1922.
———. "Held Under Heavy Bail: Frank Rice Must Face U.S. Grand Jury." March 12, 1909.
———. "Illegally in United States." March 12, 1909.
———. "Indictment Brought In." April 9, 1909.
———. Local correspondence regarding body snatchers. April 23, 1869.
———. "Mooney Electrocuted." May 6, 1904.
———. Note regarding Abraham Terrier. December 11, 1908.
———. Note regarding Abraham Terrier. August 15, 1916.
———. Note regarding gypsies in Upper Jay. June 12, 1909.
———. Note regarding gypsies. July 23, 1914.
———. Note regarding houses of ill-repute. March 17, 1881.
———. Note regarding tramps. July 23, 1886.
———. Note regarding wild man near Port Henry. March 9, 1883.
———. "Our Jail Population." December 3, 1909.
———. "Rice Gets Three Years." April 16, 1909.
———. "Say She is Black Witch." July 4, 1912.
———. "Traced to LaColle." December 3, 1909.

———. "Tramps are Warned to Stay Elsewhere." June 5, 1925.
———. "Unknown Man Found Frozen at Keeseville." November 19, 1920.
———. "Veteran Horse Thief Captured." March 22, 1894.
Potsdam Herald. "Fall Island Scene of Village's First Duel; Third 'Shot' Downs Jeweler." March 16, 1950.
Potsdam Herald-Recorder. "Barney Moscow Killed." April 25, 1913.
———. "The Early History of Parishville." August 29, 1913.
Republican-Journal. "Corpse Vamoosed When Scared Watcher Ran Away." March 13, 1917.
Shor, Murray. "The Duel of Fall Island." *Courier & Freeman*, October 10, 1957.
St. Lawrence Herald. "Arrests at Jayville." August 9, 1895.
St. Lawrence Plaindealer. Note regarding Lon Clark. June 27, 1894.
St. Lawrence Republican. "Grand Jury Hears Evidence." April 14, 1909.
———. "Grave Robbers at Clayton – Attempt to Steal the Body of an Old Resident." March 2, 1898.
———. "Held in Watertown: An Ogdensburg Woman Charged with Abduction." November 18, 1903.
———. "The Jayville Outrage." August 14, 1895.
———. "Man, Walking on Tracks, Killed by Central Train." April 23, 1913.
———. "Manslaughter in Second Degree: The Charge Against Barney Moscow of Sissonville." August 6, 1902.
———. "The Maple Island Mystery." January 6, 1892.
———."A Mystery of the St. Lawrence." October 7, 1891.
———. Note regarding *People v. Barney Moscow*. November 5, 1902.
———. Note regarding witchcraft. January 13, 1904.
———. "Parents Find Their Lost Son." August 20, 1913.
———. "Sentenced by Judge Ray: Heavy Penalties Meted Out in 'White Slave' Cases." April 14, 1909.
———. "Woman is Arrested." March 3, 1909.
———. "A Woman Tarred and Feathered." August 7, 1895.
Stearns, Mena. "Grave Snatchers Have Odd Resting Place at Old Forge." *Massena Observer*, May 10, 1938.
———. "Men Who Reportedly Made Job of Grave Snatching Buried in Special Graves." *Massena Observer*, August 11, 1952.
Sunday Herald. "Madam Vespucci." August 8, 1897.
Ticonderoga Sentinel. "Hunter Reports Wild Man Deep in Forestland." December 2, 1948.
———. "Sold Into Slavery—Child Sold for 50 Cents and Traded for Chickens." December 3, 1908.

———. "The 'Wild Man'." November 13, 1941.
———. "Wild Man at Rainbow Lake." November 25, 1909.
Tupper Lake Free Press. "Three Arrested for Public Intoxication." October 23, 1941.
Tupper Lake Herald. Locals regarding wild man. October 22, 1915.
Watertown Herald. "Brevities." August 26, 1916.
———. "A Jayville Elopement." June 1, 1895.
———. "Neat Work of Fortune-Tellers." August 1, 1908.
———. Note regarding body snatchers. February 26, 1898.
———. Note regarding Steen Ferguson. November 13, 1897.
Watertown Re-Union. "After Gypsies Who Stole Boy." August 23, 1913.
———. "Arrests at Jayville." August 7, 1895.
———. "County Court Opens: Trial of Anna Hazzard on Charge of Abduction." June 22, 1904.
———. "Eloped from Jayville." May 29, 1895.
———. "Headed for Syracuse. Party of Gypsies Driven Out of Jefferson County." October 22, 1907.
———. "In the County Court." March 12, 1904.
———. "In the County Court: Anna Hazzard Given Six Months in County Jail." June 25, 1904.
———. "Kidnapped Boy Found by Photo." August 29, 1913.
———. "Lost Watch and $80 at Carthage." February 25, 1905.
———. Note regarding Bert Covey. November 23, 1901.
———. Note regarding gypsies in Antwerp. July 22, 1908.
———. "A Ruined Hut's Secret." July 25, 1896.
———. "Thieves Open a Grave." March 2, 1898.
———. "Will Be Deported." August 14, 1909.

ONLINE SOURCES

"Apoplexy." Wikipedia, the free encyclopedia. http://en.wikipedia.org/wiki/Apoplexy.
"Biography of Adventurer Elena America Vespucci Part 2." Trivia-Library.com. www.trivia-library.com/b-biography-of-adventurer-elena-america-vespucci-part-2.htm.
"Body snatching." Wikipedia, the free encyclopedia. http://en.wikipedia.org/wiki/Body_snatching.
"Clayton (town), New York." Wikipedia, the free encyclopedia. http://en.wikipedia.org/wiki/Clayton_(town),_New_York.

"Duel." Wikipedia, the free encyclopedia. http://en.wikipedia.org/wiki/Duel.

Gooley, Lawrence P. "Saranac Lake: The Allan Mooney Murder." Adirondack Almanack. www.adirondackalmanack.com/2010/09/saranac-lake-allan-mooney-murder.html.

"Gypsies." Good Magic. http://www.goodmagic.com/carny/gypsies.htm.

"Gypsy Americans." Every Culture. http://www.everyculture.com/multi/Du-Ha/Gypsy-Americans.html.

"Gypsy Lore—Gypsies History, Rom History, Fortune Telling, Holocaust." Gypsy Advice. http://www.gypsyadvice.com/gypsy_lore.htm.

"Knights of the Golden Circle." Wikipedia, the free encyclopedia. http://en.wikipedia.org/wiki/Knights_of_the_Golden_Circle.

"Sons of Liberty." Wikipedia, the free encyclopedia. http://en.wikipedia.org/wiki/Sons_of_Liberty.

"Tarring and Feathering." Wikipedia, the free encyclopedia. http://en.wikipedia.org/wiki/Tarring_and_feathering.

About the Author

Author Cheri Farnsworth and Coco.
Photograph by Jamie Revai.

Cheri Farnsworth has written the following titles (some under the name of Cheri Revai): *Haunted Northern New York* (vols. 1–4, 2002–10); *Haunted Massachusetts* (2005); *Haunted New York* (2005); *Haunted Connecticut* (2006); *Haunted New York City* (2008); *The Big Book of New York Ghost Stories* (2009); *Haunted Hudson Valley* (2010); *Adirondack Enigma: The Depraved Intellect and Mysterious Life of North Country Wife Killer Henry Debosnys* (2010); *Murder and Mayhem in St. Lawrence County* (2010); *Alphabet Killer: The True Story of the Double Initial Murders* (2010); and *Murder and Mayhem in Jefferson County* (2011). She enjoys researching regional history, true crime and the connection between history, crime and the paranormal. Farnsworth, an accounting clerk by day and an author by night, lives in St. Lawrence County with her husband, four daughters and a menagerie of pets.

Visit us at
www.historypress.net

This title is also available as an e-book